Marriage Made Easy

It Doesn't Have to be That Hard

Steven Zimmerman

Melisa Zimmerman

BRIDGE
BUILDER

First Edition of "Marriage Made Better," by
Steven & Melisa Zimmerman
Published by Bridge Builder Ministry in 2023

Soft Cover ISBN: 978-0-9993764-5-4
eBook ISBN: 978-0-9993764-6-1

Foreword

You have probably all heard that marriage is hard work. Maybe you have even experienced a marriage where it seems like you never can quite achieve the marriage you've always wanted. That's why we are here. We have spent the last decade working with couples from all stages of marriage to help them live in a marriage that brings them joy and helps them support the other marriages they encounter.

In this book, Marriage Made Easy, you will discover by learning and applying a few simple tools, you can have a marriage that thrives. Marriage may be work, but it doesn't have to be hard work. Conflict will now become the indicator of just how well you are using the tools you learn in this book.

Imagine, if you will, a marriage where conflict is the exception and not the rule. A great marriage is one in which you both feel loved. You have your needs met, and you know what to do when the two of you disagree. Does this sound impossible? Well, trust us. It isn't.

Let me share with you what one of the many clients we have worked with has said about his marriage when he learned and applied these simple but powerful tools.

Last year my wife and I went through the worst time ever in our marriage. She left and said she wasn't coming back. We were heading for a divorce. We had come to a point in our lives where we argued constantly, we were living selfishly, and we were damaging our relationships with our two sons.

I had slowly begun drowning my regrets, sorrows, and depression at the bottom of a bottle of alcohol. I started pushing my wife and children farther and farther away and became an angry, dark, and hateful husband and father. I was at rock bottom, felt completely helpless, and didn't know what to do. I made a last-ditch effort and asked my wife if she would consider trying counseling. She said, "Yes!"

I called the only person I could think of who might know where we could seek marriage counseling, the pastor of the church we attended maybe once every two or three months. He gave me the number to the Bridge Builder Ministry. I called Steve and Melisa. It was the best thing that ever happened to our marriage. To make a long story short, fast forward to today in our lives.

We just celebrated our 19th wedding anniversary and our family has been radically transformed. My wife and I are best friends again because we learned how to communicate, cherish, and love each other all over again. Melisa and Steve taught us so many things that gave us a foundation to build on.

Whether you are at the end of your rope and your marriage seems hopeless, or if you guys are doing okay but have a few issues you cannot work through, they can help you. Not only did they help my marriage, but I also learned to let go of things I didn't know I had been holding onto since as far back as my childhood. Through Melisa and Steve and their ministry, my wife and I are the freest and happiest we have ever been. I am fairly certain both our minister and Jesus are happy with us, too.

As you take the journey through Marriage Made Easy, we believe you will find simple and practical things you can start doing immediately to take your marriage to the next level. Whether your marriage is on the ropes or is a good marriage, the next level awaits.

So, jump in, enjoy the book, walk through the workbook, and see just how exceptional a marriage can be. We believe your best days of being married are ahead of you. You can succeed and thrive in marriage. Marriage can be easy. It doesn't have to be that hard.

Let's do this!

– Steve & Melisa Zimmerman

Preface

In a time when the market is saturated with self-help books, podcasts, and YouTube channels, how do you determine which is going to be right for you? Not everything out there is working. If it were, we wouldn't be in a society where over fifty percent of all marriages end in divorce. God laid out a successful blueprint for marriage. Christ and the church lived that out, which is why our primary source of information is the Bible.

Many people would argue that learning from a book written over 2000 years ago isn't relevant to society today. We share life lessons learned right here in the 21st century from our marriage that have survived death, drugs, trust violations, and division. We have come out on the other side stronger and more committed than before.

We are called to share what we learned from those experiences with you. We also share lessons learned from actual marriages that are experiencing success. Real success is not to be confused, in any shape or form with perfection.

A strong and successful marriage does not need to become extinct. We believe there can be a reverse in the current statistics, and it starts by getting the big things right and dealing with serious issues before you ever say, "I do." However, if this book finds you already married, or even remarried, you will find it helpful for you, too.

When problems come up and believe us, they will. You will be armed with the tools and techniques you need to successfully deal with them. Instead of a marriage being shaken to the core by a problem that seems too big, you wind up with a relationship that is stronger because of a God who is big enough for anything you will encounter.

This book offers information with practical applications. It provides relevant questions that stir up conversations about hot-button topics that can turn into marriage-threatening issues. If you are aware of the traps before you get to them, and have already developed plans to handle them, you increase your likelihood of successfully navigating those traps.

Communication is vital to any healthy marriage. Nine out of ten couples who come to us for counseling say their primary issue is communication. As you read the book and answer the questions for each chapter in the accompanying workbook, you develop lines of communication that, if maintained, will be the life of a healthy and successful marriage.

This book helps you recognize marriage doesn't have to be that hard, and by building a stronger foundation for your marriage or establishing an initial foundation of a God-centered marriage, you can win at marriage.

Add to that, the foundation topics of his and her needs, love languages, conflict resolution, sex and intimacy, money, kids, family, and affair-proofing your marriage, then this book, Marriage Made Easy, will lead you to a place where you discover marriage is work, but it doesn't have to be hard work.

Chapter 1

A God-Centered Marriage

What does a God-centered marriage mean? What does a God-centered marriage look like? These questions can be answered by looking at why God created marriage. In **Genesis 2:24,** we see God created marriage to be between one man and one woman. *"That is why a man leaves his father and mother and is united to his wife, and they become one flesh."*

God created marriage for many reasons, many of which we are confident we haven't even discovered yet. Let's look at three reasons God created marriage. First, for relationships. God is a relational God, and he made us in his image; second, to populate the earth (in **Genesis,** God says to "multiply"); and third, to be a type and shadow of Christ and the church.

Colossians 3:23 tells us that *"everything we do should be done as unto the Lord."* Therefore, to have a God-centered

1

marriage, we choose to love our spouse according to the plan laid out for us in the Bible as an act of worship and obedience to God. When this serves as the primary focus in marriage, it allows God to bless the marriage. By making your marriage an act of obedience and worship it switches your focus from what your spouse is doing for you, to what you are doing for God.

When we first met, Melisa and I lived several states apart. We spent hours on the telephone every day. This generally would not start until after 9 p.m. Some nights, when we did our daily Bible study and prayer, our prayer would be interrupted by someone snoring. Not that the prayers were not heartfelt and passionate. It was just really late. Had we been focused on each other's actions, or should we say inaction, we could have been offended, but we were focused on God. We still laugh about it to this day. That is one example of what a God-centered marriage looks like.

A God-centered marriage will always have the stated goal that we will not make any decisions apart from the Word of God and the leading of the Holy Spirit. This means all major relationship decisions will be driven specifically by what the Word of God says or by Biblical principles. However, minor decisions, such as coffee, tea, or soda, can be made independently.

Jesus told his disciples, *"I only speak what the Father says to me"* (**John 12:50**). It was this one singular act of devotion to God's word by Jesus that enabled Him to live a perfect life and fulfill His divine purpose on Calvary. If we embrace this philosophy, then our lives will be free of a lot of unnecessary frustration.

All too often, we choose to speak and act in ways that are driven by our hurt, emotions, or desires rather than speaking and acting in a way that brings God glory. This one simple principle, when applied to every decision, every word, and every action, will change your life and your relationship forever.

How close are you and your spouse to an agreement on this? Where are the differences? Go forward, keeping in mind that every child is born a blank slate both about God and about marriage. What we learn, we learn from the people around us. What we learn about marriage is what we see modeled by our family. In most cases, we become a spouse similar to our parents. If that is something extremely negative, we will become the opposite of what we saw in our parents. Because of this, we must be very deliberate in our efforts to become what the Bible says we should be as husbands and wives.

If you came from a godly home where your parents showed a godly marriage, this will be much easier. If you did not, then it will take much more effort and study to develop the type of marriage prescribed by the Bible. This effort will be rewarded with a higher likelihood of success. One hundred percent of the people who are married God's way are successful one hundred percent of the time. Take some time and think about what you learned from your family about marriage.

Daily Bible Study

Daily Bible study will build the foundation necessary for a successful marriage and is an essential part of a God-centered marriage. We should do this both individually and as a couple every day. We could not study more differently, but we are both intentional about studying daily. When you spend time in the Word of God daily, you open the opportunity for God to speak to you through His word. Just as food is essential for our physical body to maintain health, daily Bible study is vital for our spiritual health. When couples spend time in Bible study together, their spiritual health improves.

This doesn't have to be a long and exhaustive process every day. Our son says, "You don't have to read the Bible all day, you just have to read it every day." Sometimes a simple study using a devotional or a few Bible verses can be very impactful. Whether it is on paper, YouVersion, or through a streaming service, you can make time.

One day, we had a busy day going from work to watch a double-header baseball game played by our boys. We realized on the way that we had not done our Bible study for the day, and we did not have a Bible in the car with us. Back in the day, our phones were barely literate and could by no stretch of means be called "smart phones." We could not access the Bible on our phones. After choosing the always popular memory verse, **John 11:35** *"Jesus wept,"* we spent the next 30 minutes talking about Jesus' humanity and compassion.

God will always honor your time and dedication to Him by showing up.

Prayer

Prayer is direct communication with God. It is a powerful tool in a personal relationship with God. **Ephesians 6:18** states prayer is a part of the "Armor of God." *"Pray in the Spirit on all occasions with all kinds of prayers and requests. With this in mind, be alert and always keep on praying for all the Lord's people."* (**NIV**) There is nothing more powerful than a couple praying in agreement. With the man in place as the spiritual leader of the home, his prayer over his wife will help ensure that unity is maintained. When couples make prayer time together a priority, they form intimacy between them and God, which makes His amazing power available to them.

Frequently, we have worked with couples who both admit they pray for their spouse. However, when we ask the other spouse what their spouse prays for them, they rarely know. Praying out loud for your spouse so they can hear you, brings unity and encouragement to your spouse. We teach our couples to pray a prayer of blessing over their spouse out loud so their spouse can hear them every day.

What is a prayer of blessing? The process for praying for your spouse is not a prescribed prayer. It's simply inviting God to bless your spouse. It doesn't have to be deep and theological or even contain a single scripture reference, it just needs to be sincere from the heart asking God to do something good for your spouse. There is almost no way to get this wrong. As long as you are asking God to bless your spouse and not tossing in a few requests for God to change your spouse, then you are good.

This is not the time to subtly let your spouse know what they are doing is bothering you. It's simply a time of inviting God to work in their lives to bring good things to them. This simple 1-3-minute prayer, prayed with your spouse, out loud, and then reciprocated by the other person, is authentically one of the most powerful things you can do to build intimacy in your marriage.

In **Matthew 18:19,** the Bible says, *"When two or more shall agree concerning anything you ask in prayer, it will be done for you."* It is exceedingly difficult to have a conflict with someone you are praying for and/or praying with you every day. We routinely pray together at the end of the day. Having a set time helps ensure we get it in every day.

Occasionally, we have found ourselves in conflict at the end of the day. Even if the conflict hasn't been completely resolved, it doesn't mean we just end the day without our regular prayer time. As you can imagine, we have ended the day, on more than one occasion, praying our prayer of blessing for the other person through clenched teeth. It has proven to be an effective way to prevent "the sun from going down on your anger." Starting and ending the day praying together is a vital part of a healthy relationship.

Remember, ultimately, you will win or lose as a team. If

you are establishing a new pattern of adding prayer to your marriage, it will take both of you to be successful. Many times, we have asked couples to pray the blessing prayer every day with their spouse. We remind the husbands God has placed them as the spiritual leader of their homes and ideally, it would be his responsibility to lead the prayer time. However, we also remind the wives, since they are a team, they will also share in the responsibility of ensuring prayer happens.

Occasionally, though, when the couple returns to the office for their next counseling session, we will ask them how they did with the prayer time. Frequently, the wife will respond, annoyed, "We didn't pray." When questioned about why they didn't pray, she would respond, "Well, I was waiting for him to lead the prayer because you told him he was the spiritual leader and he never did."

Ladies, please remember, you can probably have what you want by simply being a team player. If you get to the end of the day and your husband hasn't initiated prayer time, simply look at him and say, "Do you mind if I pray for you?" Then just pray for him. Guys, here is the hint, if she says that to you, remember, a smart husband will say, "Honey, I would love that, but let me pray for you first." Guys, you become the hero, and success is at hand. This is a simple practice that, when added to your marriage, will create so much positive momentum that you will wonder why you didn't do it all along.

The Three-Stranded Cord

Ecclesiastes 4:12 says, *"Though one may be overpow-ered, two can defend themselves. A cord of three strands is not easily broken."* This passage of scripture illustrates the impor-tance of the covenant relationship between a husband and wife and that their relationship is intertwined with God. This causes the strands to become one cord, which is not only difficult to break, but is very difficult to separate.

Many of the greatest bridges in the world support extremely heavy weight by wrapping cables around each other, whether it is the Golden Gate, the George Washington, or the Brooklyn Bridge, they use this principle. This symbol of a God-centered marriage serves as a reminder that God's love will continue to bind you together as one for the entirety of your marriage.

Another great reminder we receive from the three-stranded cord is if one cord becomes stressed or frayed, the other strands will ensure the cord remains intact, giving the stressed or frayed cord time to heal. Even in those times in a marriage when both partners are stressed or at their breaking point, God will hold the marriage together as each person works to regain whole-ness. The Lord's strand cannot be broken, and He can hold the cord together as long as the other cords do not separate them-selves from Him.

In our second year of marriage, I (Melisa) had just lost my mom after a lengthy battle with breast cancer. I was very close to my mother. We had been living with her and my dad for several weeks before her death. This brought me to one of the lowest times in my life. I felt depressed and even angry with God for not healing my mom.

For many weeks following my mom's death, I was not only disengaged from life, but I was also mostly disengaged from my marriage. In the place of brokenness, it would have been easy for Steven to become frustrated and upset with me. However, his dedication and focus on God kept him in a place where he could provide the support I needed to heal.

This is our favorite picture of the "three-strand cord" in our marriage. There have been other times when Steven was in a low place or struggling with an issue in life, and I could support and encourage him by remaining in a place of focus on God for our marriage. Even if you find both of you are in a low place at the same time, this is the place, you will see God holding both of you together as you continue to maintain your relationship with Him.

One of our favorite scriptures is **2 Corinthians 12:9a**. *"The Lord said to me, 'My grace is sufficient for you, for My power is made perfect in weakness.'"* Paul tells the people at Corinth that, in his times of weakness, God's power is made perfect in him. We can have this confidence that even when both spirits are lagging, God will hold us together.

Team Names

What is a team name, and why do we need one? This is a name you choose together for you and your spouse or future spouse. It simply helps us remember an important key - we are on the same team. We're teammates, not opponents. When things felt like we were opponents, we could recognize this as an attempt by Satan to cause division.

The Enemy loves division. How easy his job becomes if he can get us to take each other down. If he can get us to be destructive towards each other, nit-pick, say critical and inaccurate things about each other's motives, and have a negative or hurtful perception of the other... if he can get us to help him with his job, then he has gained a foothold in our lives. If he can get us to act more like we are on his team than our spouse's team... "Yikes!"

The Bible presents these truths in **Ephesians 6:12**:

"For our struggle is not against flesh and blood, but against the rulers, against the authorities, against the powers of this dark world, and against the spiritual forces of evil in the heavenly realms."

Your enemy is not your spouse. Your enemy is sin and Satan. There is such strength in a united husband, wife, and the Lord! Those three strands, united as a team, create an alliance, solidarity, and strength unmatched by anything else!

So, we commit to:

- *"Be alert and of a sober mind. Your enemy the devil prowls around like a roaring lion looking for someone to devour."* (**1 Peter 5:8**)

By choosing to stay alert, we commit to team unity and achieving goals to help us move through every situation with unity and strength. With courage and fortitude, we defeat all inklings of accusation or blame, and we keep the devil from gaining a foothold in our lives!

- *"Therefore, what God has joined together, let no one separate"* (**Mark 10:9**)

Amen!! In the strength and solidity of the Lord, commitment to a team mindset enables wonderful victory!

Every couple, even those who have been together for even a brief period, have some sort of inside joke and a "shared story" that often provides a perfect opportunity to give birth to your team's name. The best team names are going to evoke pleasant memories and smiles every time we mention them and will serve as a warm reminder of why you got married. It will also remind you of the value of your marriage to each other and to the Lord.

Because we are sure you are asking, "So, Mr. & Mrs. Perfect, what's your team's name?" Our team's name is the awe-inspiring, "Cake Toppers." We know you are on the edge of your seat with anticipation, wondering just how we could come up with such an inspirational team name.

Here is our story: God planted in us a dream of marriage ministry early in our relationship. We dreamed about it, prayed about it, and pursued what we believed God was calling us to do. However, given my (Melisa's) unsuccessful 20-year marriage, this seemed sort of a stretch for us. As we continued to follow the dream, God revealed the concept of the wedding cake and how it could teach about marriage and relationships.

Most people remember the dress and cake at a wedding. The bride and groom stand at the top of the cake. The cake-topper symbolizes the bride and the groom at their closest together. Because being in unity is so vital to a marriage, we chose the name "Cake Toppers." It is a silly name that is frequently used to bring a smile to the other person or encouragement in a tough time or just as a conversation point to teach others about marriage.

There you go! The abridged version of how we became this team. "Go Cake-Toppers!!" One of the fun things we have done is collect cake topper items. I (Melisa) have a charm bracelet with not 1 but 2 cake topper charms. Little things like these charms keep in the forefront of our minds that we are "Cake Toppers." Our common motto is "Cake Toppers ALWAYS win!" With this idea in mind, work together to find your team's great name.

Chapter 2

BANG for the Buck: Love Languages

We are not so proud to think we are the only ones with great ideas about how to have a good marriage. This brings us to the heart of this chapter, The 5 Love Languages. The 5 Love Languages is a book written by Gary Chapman over 20 years ago. It is great! This chapter is largely one giant footnote.

It is so good, and so important, that we teach it to every couple regardless of the state of their relationship. It is so important that before we ever got together as a couple, I (Steven) received a copy of The 5 Love Languages and was asked to read it. I (Steve) was frantically reading the last pages as Melisa came down the escalator at the baggage claim, in the Minneapolis/St. Paul International Airport when I saw her in person for the first time.

We keep copies of this book in our office to give to couples who are unfamiliar with the material. This chapter is just an appetizer for the Five Love Languages book. The main course is for you to go out and buy the book, read it, and put into practice everything the book talks about.

Everyone has a love tank. Think gas tank for your car. For a car to run, there has to be gas in the tank. For it to run well, it has to be the right gas. There needs to be plenty of gas in the love tank for a marriage to run well. There are, and let there be no doubt about it, long stretches between gas stations in your relationship. However, this should not be the case. Just like your car needs frequent fill-ups, so does your love tank and your spouse's as well.

I (Steve) once borrowed my son's high-end pickup truck, as I had loaned my car to a friend. I was driving to our friend's house straight from work. When I left work, I noticed the truck was low on fuel. I did the responsible thing and stopped to put some gasoline in it. Yes, gas. I didn't use diesel fuel even though I was driving a DIESEL truck.

I was lucky it didn't die on the highway. When it came time to move my son's truck to make room for another car, it voiced its displeasure at my choice. Oddly enough, it didn't run well on the wrong fuel. The result was we had to pull out the fuel tank, empty it, clean it, put it back in and add some diesel. This goes to show the value of adding the right fuel.

Many couples we see have one or both of them thinking they are crushing it, and they can't figure out why everything isn't coming up roses. You can have two people working hard at a marriage, but if they are putting the wrong fuel in each other's love tank, the results will not be good. You are going to wind up with two exhausted and unhappy people who feel unloved.

We advocate the motto, "Love Smarter, not Harder." Hence, the title of this book, "Marriage Made Easy: It doesn't have to be that hard." Using the right fuel goes a long way towards creating a happy marriage.

There are five basic ways people give and receive love. We all do all of them. We operate better and more easily in some of them and not so well when using the others. There are primary languages and secondary languages for each of us. Our experience with couples is that the top two love languages get meaningful results for people. We are going to look at each of them individually.

Often, husbands and wives don't share primary and secondary love languages. It is incumbent on you to become fluent in your spouse's love languages, even if it is not natural to you. We struggled with this early on. Our first big fight occurred on the eve of our wedding.

Melisa, whose primary love language is Gifts, put a great deal of time and thought into a wedding gift. Let it be noted, Steve didn't even buy her a gift. My (Steve) response to her gift was to do what my mother taught me to say. "Thank you." This was not celebrating the act of giving like a person with Gifts as their love language, wants, and needs.

The flip side of the Love Languages coin is that once cell phones advanced to making texts easier than hitting a button three times to get to the letter C, I (Steve) blew up Melisa's phone with compliments. She did not celebrate it as an outpouring of affection, but an interruption of her day. Eventually, God told Melisa, "Maybe Steven would like you to say something back."

We are not advocating you to change who you are so you can better love your spouse. It is about understanding where they are coming from and doing your best to meet them there. Learning to both speak your spouse's love language and remind yourself that when they are speaking their Love Language to you, they are still showing your love is a vital part of sharing and feeling.

Let's look at the 5 Love Languages individually.

Physical Touch

Let's be clear right off the bat. Physical touch is not sex. People confuse the two and it leads to a Physical Touch person feeling neglected. This would seem to be the easiest language to satisfy, but it is often neglected.

This occurs a lot in marriages where the couples have been married for quite some time. The arrival and demands of newborns, infants, and small kids frequently hurt or at least puts a dent in this language. I (Melisa) recognize that if the babies are treating you like a public utility, and the toddlers are attached to your leg like velcro, it can deplete your desire to cuddle.

However, if your husband's love language is Physical Touch, then their need doesn't go away because your desire for physical touch is depleted. Recognizing this is vital to keep your husband's Physical Touch love tank full.

The wonderful thing about touch is that it is free. You can fulfill this language regardless of your standard of living. The second outstanding feature of touch is you, with a little effort, can get it right every single time. I (Steve) grew up in a family where everyone hugged each other. It took 20 minutes to say goodbye because everyone needed to be hugged before you left.

Melisa grew up in a home that was the exact opposite. They never touched each other. The difference was never starker than when we went over to Melisa's parents, and I (Steve) went to hug her mom. I was told, "Steve, love me from over there" as she pointed across the room. It took a long time for me to adjust. Adjustment was done by everyone involved. Melisa has a much lower need for contact, but that doesn't lessen my desire to "get it right."

Simple conversations can lead to much more effective loving smarter, not harder. The act of putting your hand on your spouse's leg while you drive or giving them a peck on the head when you get up to get something to drink goes a long way to speaking physical touch. I (Steve) learned that touching is welcomed, but rubbing is not. Circling my thumb often was met with, "You're rubbing a hole in me." Heard. Received. Acted upon.

Love in a way that is received by your husband/wife. This

is what we mean by learning your brand of touch isn't always the same brand as your spouse, but if you learn and make necessary adjustments, you can always do what your spouse enjoys and what fills their Physical Touch love tank.

Gifts

Who doesn't love birthdays and Christmas? The answer is nobody. Some people love them more than others. Gifts people express love through the giving and receiving of gifts. I (Melisa) am a proud Gifts person as most of my family and friends know. I give highly thoughtful gifts and hope to receive the same.

It is not the price of the gift that matters. Although I won't turn down diamonds or vacations, it is the amount of effort and consideration that went into it that makes the biggest impact on me. For me, it's the idea that you thought of me and took the step to get something for me that is the love part of having Gifts as my love language.

There is a learning curve that can take place with gifts as well. I (Melisa) love flowers. When I was young, I worked in a flower shop. I work hard in my front flower bed. On my first birthday as a married couple, Steve started giving gifts for all seven days of my birthday week. This was great. He brought me a dozen roses, also good. (A dozen roses in a vase are even better.) Once I explained the benefits of vases, we didn't have

an issue. Love smarter, not harder. Flowers in vases are a no fuss, no muss solution.

The misconception is that Gifts people are all about receiving gifts. They are as much about giving them. You need to celebrate their gift journey when they give something to you. Chances are, they put a lot of thought into it. I (Melisa) bought Steve a beautiful turtleneck sweater just because. It did not impress him. We went back and forth about why he should like it more and it nearly caused a fight. The good news is that he's gotten so many compliments on it that the sweater is now one of his favorites. I was hurt by how he received my gift.

When a Gifts person gives a gift and it is met with a nonchalant or critical attitude, it is like saying, "I don't love you." to the person giving the gift. While it is not crucial that you start a parade complete with a marching band and cheerleaders every time you get a gift, you must recognize, and then convey, that you have received the love that was just shared with you. Also, remember it is not so much the cost of the gift as it is that you thought enough of them and made the effort to give them something. Sometimes a drink and snack conveys love just as well as an extravagant gift.

Quality Time

We find the secret here in the name. Everyone has time, and if you're married or in a committed relationship, you are going to spend time together. Quality time is meaningful, eye-to-eye time. You are the center of my attention kind of time. Washing dishes together is NOT quality time. It may be the love language of Acts of Service, but it is not necessarily Quality Time. We cover that in a little bit.

I (Steven) am a quality-time person. Melisa is both a wonderful cook and a gifted hostess. Early on, Melisa would have a dozen people over for dinner and games and think this is great. We are together, all our friends are around, and time gets no more quality than this. She is a superb hostess, and she talks and connects with all her guests. This meant she wasn't talking to me.

This is a classic disconnect for people in relationships with quality-time people. My wife is a quick learner. She later took me on an amazing birthday trip to Tulsa. It was hours in the car just talking, riding scooters, going to a live performance, and throwing axes. There were no kids, grandkids, or friends. It was just us for the entire weekend, doing fun things.

It was on that trip that Melisa discovered the magic of road trips. There is not much that I (Steve) like better than tasty food, good times, and my wife all to myself. It fills my love tank. She has wisely re-used this highly successful strategy because she is smart. Love smarter – not harder. It doesn't have to be that hard.

Speaking of doing fun things, let's talk about cell phones for a second; nothing robs Quality Time like being with the person you love, and they are lost in their phone. Mutual phone time is fine, but you are not putting anything in the love tank if you say,

"We spent four hours together last night," when you used that time to clear 12 levels on Candy Crush.

The receiver of the gift of time must be receptive. An example of this is when we go out to eat. I (Steve) will sit facing the doorway. This prevents me from being distracted by sports on television. I can then receive love and have my tank filled by my wife trying to love me in my language.

Acts of Service

This is doing something above and beyond to show love for your spouse. I (Melisa) have this as my secondary language. There is a difference between doing your share and performing an act of service. An act of service is usually something that is not part of a task list. Washing clothes and doing dishes are something that just needs to be done. You may get half credit for those. Everyone wears clothing and eats food. It can be a task you don't want to do and your spouse does it because they love you. We have a couple of things that fall into this category.

We have had dogs, large ones, for most of our marriage. They can make a mess out of a backyard. Steve has been kind enough to take care of the worst part of dog ownership for me for years. Pumping gas is something I (Melisa) can do myself, but would rather not. Steve does it as an act of service. These are little things, but they mean the world to me and make me feel loved.

There are, of course, larger things, like cleaning the garage.

I enjoy a clean garage. This is something for which he gets a month of bonus points every time I park my car. Acts of Service, like all the love languages, are better if you have a conversation with your spouse about the things that will get meaningful results, making them feel loved... and the things that do not. Nothing is worse than busting your butt to do acts of service and not get credit for them because they aren't the acts your spouse sees as important and loving. Learn what speaks love and do the things that move the needle. Love smarter - not harder.

Words of Affirmation

On a basic level, everyone needs to be encouraged. For Words of Affirmation people, this is twice as important and can give the husband/wife twice the credit for loving well. This can be both the easiest and the hardest language to master. If you have grown up in a performance-based love environment, you have learned we reward actions more than words... and you can struggle with this. If compliments come naturally to you, you will find you can knock this one out of the park with little effort.

I (Melisa) will tell you, for me, Words of Affirmation are 7 out of 5 when it comes to these Love Languages. This presented a challenge since it is Steven's #1 language. He would blow up my phone with texts telling me how wonderful I am. I would look at it and think, "That's nice," and get on with the rest of my day. One day, after my sixth or seventh text, God spoke to my heart and said, "He would like you to say something back." I thought to myself, "I've got nothing." However, I knew I needed to learn this foreign language.

I Googled, "Nice things to say to your husband." I searched ideas on Pinterest, and asked several of my Words of Affirmation friends, "What are things you would like your husband to say to you?" Then I loaded some of these 'Words of Affirmation' into my phone and set a timer to remind me to send them to him. Some people say, "Well, that's not very romantic. That's not from the heart." Truth is, I got bonus points because Steven knew I was going out of my comfort zone to learn how to love him well.

You do not have to lie to provide words of affirmation. If your spouse is lazy, don't tell them they are such a hard worker. You can let them know they are a good listener or have great hair. You find that, like so many other things, the more you put it into practice, the easier it gets. I (Melisa) have gotten quite good at paying my husband compliments, even though I used to be bad at it. You, too, can find success with words of affirmation, as you can with any other love language, by practicing daily.

The other great thing about speaking the Words of Affirmation language is its free and you can do it any time in person when you are with your spouse, or by text or email if you are not with them. As long as you are sincere, you can never speak this language too much.

Hopefully, laying out the 5 Love Languages will help you execute 'The Big Three, making God the center of your marriage, meeting each other's needs, and giving and receiving love effectively. We believe this is a cornerstone principle. Everyone who reads our book should buy Dr. Chapman's book for a more comprehensive understanding of this essential idea.

Dr. Chapman's ministry has also put out an app we have found very helpful for many couples. The app, 'The Love Nudge', helps you by connecting you with your spouse (you both need to have the app for it to work), and by setting up reminders to love your spouse in their love language.

We have been speaking each other's love language for nearly 20 years and we still enjoy using the app to keep us loving in their love language regularly. Try it. I bet you will like it too.

Chapter 3

We All Have Needs! His Needs

Having a loving and satisfying marriage is one of the best blessings we can have. There is nothing more peaceful and powerful than a husband and wife who love each other and meet each other's needs. When you understand the needs of your spouse, you can then identify ways to meet his/her needs. This is an essential component of a successful marriage.

When a spouse's needs go unmet, the likelihood of an affair increases. Statistics say half of all marriages will experience infidelity. Despite these stats, we must say there is never any excuse for an affair. It is important to remember that Satan operates in Unmet Needs. The devil hates marriage because it is so sacred to God. Too many people take the energy God gives them to love each other and use it to change the other person.

When you reject your spouse's needs, you reject your spouse. God's design created you differently.

Men and women have basic needs. These needs are typically true of most men and most women. There is no way to speak to all the shades of gray in the needs area. In this book, we will speak in generalities.

While needs are vital, we must view them through the proper lens. We don't view our spouse's needs through a lens of selfishness in our relationship with ourselves. We view them outwardly toward meeting the needs of our spouse. Jesus said, *"I came not to be served but to serve."* (**Matthew 20:28**). This approach is healthy and promotes growth in relationships.

We have often found that when teaching about the needs of a man and a woman, this knowledge is used as the measuring stick for whether someone's spouse is meeting their needs. We don't throw this out there so you can use your needs to play Whack-A-Mole with your spouse.

This is completely backward from the way this insight should be used. We must ONLY use this insight as the knowledge we have to make sure WE are meeting the needs of our spouse. By looking at this information from the wrong vantage point, you are setting yourself up for significant problems.

It is important to identify the needs of each person. We will start with the four basic needs of men. These needs are respect, sex, fellowship, and domestic support. Each of these needs is vital, and when a wife is meeting all the needs of her spouse, she is not only ensuring a good relationship, but she is following the pattern set out in the Bible.

The first and primary need of a man is Respect

Ephesians 5:33 says, *"But this also applies to you; every husband must love his wife as himself and **every wife must respect her husband**"* (emphasis added). Respect looks different for men than it does for women. When women disrespect men, it is especially hurtful and undermining and will lead to an emotional distance that creates long-term problems.

What men view as disrespect is usually something women do not. For example, telling a joke to your friends where your husband is the object of ridicule, or something he did that provides the humor for the joke, is very disrespectful to men. Women often just see it as something funny. Correcting your spouse in front of others is very disrespectful as well, while most women just see it as being helpful. Criticizing his work performance or ability to generate income is also another area where women can be perceived as being very disrespectful.

I (Melisa) used to struggle badly in this area. Before discovering how important it was, I had bought a car without consulting my husband. When he confronted me about this blatant show of disrespect, my response was even worse. I replied, "Why does it matter? You aren't going to pay for it, anyway." I couldn't have come up with a poorer response if I'd tried. These are just a few ways men and women view disrespect differently.

Another way wives are disrespectful to their husbands is by talking over them, finishing their sentences, or correcting them as they are talking or telling a story. While this is perfectly acceptable to women, with men you should NEVER do this. Learning to allow your husband to finish his thought without interrupting him is a well-learned skill. (This works for all guys, no matter their age.)

Let us look at one more way our wives get respectfulness wrong. Repeat after me ladies, "I am not my husband's mother. I never have been and I never will be." No matter where your husband is in life, if his mother is living or not, you will NEVER be his mother.

Mothering comes so naturally for most women. They 'mom' others without even being aware of it. We have had too many guys come in for marriage counseling and say, "I don't want to be just another one of the children." Making sure you treat your husband as your partner and not your child will increase his feeling of being respected so much. A heightened awareness of disrespectful behavior is going to prevent you from unintentionally hurting your husband and damaging your relationship.

One of the best ways to identify disrespect is to ask your husband directly, "What do I do that comes across as disrespectful to you?" Word of warning: if you are not diligently looking at this to gain insight about how to improve your relationship, you can easily find yourself with your feelings hurt and feeling judged or condemned.

Men, you can use other women as an example of how to be disrespectful to your wife without directly criticizing her. Pointing out a woman at the restaurant berating the wait staff or dressing down her husband in front of the kids can help your wife identify unacceptable behavior when she sees it. This can give your wife insight into her behavior in a less confrontational way. Approaching this often-difficult conversation lovingly will help prevent unnecessary offense.

Having discussed what disrespect looks like, we need to take some time and talk about what respect looks like. There are many ways to show respect, but nothing shows respect more than a few simple words, such as, "I trust your judgment." "I know you have the best interests of our family at heart." or "I'm behind you one hundred percent." By allowing your husband to be the head of the household as instructed in the Bible, you are showing your respect for him and his position.

For some women, this is a difficult undertaking, especially if they have never seen this behavior modeled. By being diligent in studying the Word and by reading books, you will increase your knowledge and capacity to exhibit respect. If you feel you don't have time to read books, there are many great blogs you can read and follow to learn practical ways to show respect for your husband.

Women who learn how to be respectful as wives are some

of the smartest women in the world. They also have some of the best marriages.

The second most important need for men is Sex

The only thing that will surprise anyone about this section is that sex is not the most important need for men. It is, however, an important need and must be seen as that. God designs sex in marriage and it is part of a man's basic makeup. Scriptures show both the husband and wife need to be involved. Sex is not a bartering tool or a weapon, but it is designed to be an integral part of marriage. All too often, we find women use withholding sex as a manipulation tool or a punishment.

This practice goes against what is set forth in the Bible.

"The husband should fulfill his wife's sexual needs, and the wife should fulfill her husband's needs. The wife gives authority over her body to her husband, and the husband gives authority over his body to his wife. Do not deprive each other of sexual relations unless you both agree to refrain from sexual intimacy for a limited time so you can give yourselves more completely to prayer. Afterward, you should come together again so Satan won't be able to tempt you because of your lack of self-control." **(1 Corinthians 7:3-5)**

We do not intend this passage to infer that wives can never say 'No' to sex. It does, however, give us an excellent picture of what our attitude toward sex should look like. Sex was created to be mutually satisfying and when we make that our priority, sex should be something both people look forward to and enjoy. Wives, we can't have a headache every day. Also, your husband should not be the only person initiating sex.

Inside marriage, sex allows for freedom of expression, but as with any good relationship, some boundaries need to be decided on and respected. Sex should never be done in a way that causes one spouse to feel degraded or demoralized. It is a loving act, and each spouse should treat the other with the utmost respect and honor. The more boundaries are honored, the more likely they will grow and stretch with time.

Everything is better when you involve God. Because God designed sex, this is even more true in this area. You should try praying before and/or after sex. This will not only make your sex more intimate, but it will discourage one spouse from dishonoring the other person's boundaries. We will discuss sex more extensively in a later chapter.

The third need of a man is Fellowship

There is nothing better than being married to your best friend. He wants you to be interested in the things he is interested in. The wife needs to be willing to do the things he likes to do, even if it means she needs to learn more about sports, fishing, or any other interests he has. This is part of sacrificial love. This creates an environment where you can just have fun together.

Having fun is one element that keeps a marriage alive and growing and prevents it from eroding into a business relationship. I (Steven) really enjoy NASCAR. However, Melisa was not interested in watching cars go in circles for several hours at a time. She has learned enough about NASCAR to speak with some intelligence about it. She even knows about drafting, manufacturers, and pit times. Melisa can tell you my favorite driver is Denny Hamlin. He drives the number 11 FedEx Toyota Camry. She does not always get hysterical if I wear my Denny Hamlin gear to church on race day.

Not only did Melisa learn enough to have intelligent conversations about NASCAR, but she also now enjoys it. Now there will be times she asks me what time the race starts and if we have it recorded. I feel especially loved on those Sundays.

Lucky for me, Melisa grew up in a family that enjoys sports. She is knowledgeable about football and can totally hold her own when it comes to baseball. She has a good knack for calling strikes and balls and being able to identify the infield fly rule. She will not watch WWE or golf with me, but there are enough things we can enjoy together, even if they are not her favorite things.

Wives, be careful not to use this process to martyr yourself. Doing what he enjoys does not give you the license to grumble and complain about never getting to do what you want. When you do this, more out of love, the more you are going to find it returned on his behalf.

Wives, here is a friendly reminder: fully engaging with your husband in the activities he loves is not the same as just being in the same room with him and being on your phone or being disengaged while he enjoys the activity. Fully engaging and being able to have an intelligent conversation about the activity is a requirement.

Finally, the fourth basic need of a man is Domestic Support

Wives can create the environment in the home. Every man needs a comforting and welcoming environment to come home too. After being in the workplace all day, they need a place to come where they feel like they are valuable and important. Ladies, this is one area where you can shine. Even if you work outside the home, it is still a terrific opportunity to serve your husband and meet one of his basic needs. It may take some effort on your part, especially if you were not raised in this kind of environment. However, by creating a warm and welcoming home for your husband, you also create a place he wants to come home to.

This can look different to different people. You know your husband better than anyone else. He may need some space when he comes home to unwind and reboot his brain for home life, or maybe he needs to be doted on and be the center of your universe for a while. Whether he needs space or attention, almost every man loves to be greeted at the door with a warm hug and a serious kiss. Whatever creative way you find to welcome your husband home, always be willing to make his homecoming something that shows your gratefulness that he is home and your desire to meet his needs.

There is a distinction between men and women that goes hand in hand with creating a safe place. Women are physically modest. They go to the bathroom in stalls with the door shut. If the latch is broken, they pee with one foot holding the door closed. They go to the shower in health clubs wrapped in a towel. They go into the shower, pull the curtain, then hang the towel up on the hook. They then reach out, grab the towel, dry off, and go back to their locker.

Men pee in urinals next to someone they've never met before. They go to the shower at the gym with a towel... draped over their shoulder. Not a care in the world who sees what. Most of them are not ashamed of their 'dad bods'.

But most men are emotionally modest. It is hard to get them to open up about emotional issues and their insecurities (and they have a bunch of them). There have been more than one girls' lunch meetings where no one was concerned about spilling the tea.

Women, you need to be in a vault where men's emotional secrets are safe FOREVER. If you share them with your mom, sister, or bestie, and they let on that you have shared, the results will be disastrous. Your husband will clam up and getting significant 'shares' after that will become almost impossible.

Domestic support also includes such things as cooking meals, cleaning the house, and providing clean clothing for him to wear. While these seem like mundane chores, they all speak loudly about your desire to serve him. Little things, like asking what he would like for dinner or picking up after him from time to time, are thoughtful gestures that, if done consistently and out of the heart to serve him and love him, will not go unnoticed.

Proverbs 31 gives a notable example of what a godly wife looks like. It is a great passage of scripture to study and implement in your relationship with your husband. By serving him in this way, you are creating a place where not only will he want to come home to, but he will also feel very valued and honored, which is something God asks wives to do in His word.

Wives, as you make meeting these basic needs of your husband a priority and a habit, you will find your husband feels much more connected to you and will probably increase his willingness to open up emotionally to you. Nothing makes you feel more loved than having your basic needs met consistently.

Chapter 4

We All Have Needs! Her Needs

Marriage between a man and a woman and God was God's plan from the beginning. This union is the exact replication of the trinity. God refers to Christians as the Bride of Christ throughout the New Testament. As men walk out the truths of the Word, they will find they fulfill the needs of their wives. **Ephesians 5:25-26** tells husbands to love their wives as Christ loves the church and gives Himself up for her.

Having looked at men's needs in the previous chapter; we now examine the needs of women. Men's needs and women's needs are very different. This is a plan specifically designed by God. When husbands can identify and meet the needs of their wives, they find that unity becomes not only achievable, but immensely powerful as well.

Psalm 133 (TPT) beautifully captures the power of unity.

"How truly wonderful and delightful to see brothers and sisters living together in sweet unity! It's as precious as the sacred oil flowing from the head of high priest Aaron, dripping down his beard and running all the way down to the hem of his priestly robes. We can compare this heavenly harmony to the dew dripping down from the skies upon Mount Hermon, refreshing the mountain slopes of Israel. God will release his promise of life forever!"

Who doesn't want to live in God's promises?

Again, it is important to note the needs of women which we will identify in this chapter are given in generalities. There is not enough space to identify all the variations of these needs. The needs of a woman include security, affection, open communication, and leadership. This list of needs is not given to be used as a measuring stick by the wife to determine if her husband is meeting her needs, but by the husband to provide practical ways to meet the needs of his wife. It is important to keep the proper perspective when we identify and implement the needs of a woman.

The first and primary need of a woman is Security

A woman's need for security shows itself in four areas: emotional, spiritual, physical, and financial security. For a woman, emotional security is an issue of the heart. Spiritual security is a soul issue. Physical security involves touch. The basis for financial security is wrapped in provision. As a spouse meets these needs, areas of insecurity decrease tremendously, which allows her to fully enjoy marriage. A secure wife is then in a better place to meet the needs of her husband.

An example of meeting an **emotional security** need is allowing freedom of expression. A woman who can reveal her true feelings without a threat of punishment or reprisal is more emotionally secure. If she feels using her genuine emotions will cause a disturbance every time she says or responds to something from her husband, she will feel insecure.

If the husband responds negatively, and uses demeaning words, like stupid or dumb, the level of insecurity will ramp up. You can disagree without putting her down. You should not only avoid being extremely harsh but also be welcoming of her expressing her emotions. Taking the 'Not this again'! approach is going to make things emotionally unstable for her.

A husband needs to remember that women are highly charged emotional beings, and this is exactly how God created them to be. If you support your wife on an emotional level, you will find this can bring about a much more stable and secure relationship. Because men and women view emotions differently, it is easy for a husband to feel that if his wife is being emotional; she cannot think clearly or develop effective plans. However, because of the way women process their emotions, the very opposite is often the case.

Men need to be careful not to under-value emotions. Men often see emotions as a weakness, and he needs to honor emotions as an intricate part of a woman's makeup, and to deny her emotions is to deny her the emotional security she needs.

Men view things through a logical lens, leading them to discuss what they think about a matter. They review facts. They will take a more historical approach to topics. Women, on the other hand, are driven by their feelings. They will use emotive language and approach both conversation and disagreement from a vantage point of how they feel. We are not advocating switching gender roles. We just want you to operate understanding that your spouse is coming at your communication from a unique vantage point.

If a husband will share his own emotions in an honest and non-threatening manner with his wife, it will strengthen her security and the bonds that hold them together.

Spiritual security comes when a husband is engaged in the spiritual climate of the marriage. By leading his wife in spiritual activities such as prayer, Bible study, and church attendance and involvement, he is providing an atmosphere where his wife will not only feel secure but will grow in her relationship with God. Confidence in knowing you are providing spiritual security will cause your wife to be more connected to you and to God.

A 'flash-in-the-pan' kind of relationship can not achieve spiritual security with God. To achieve true security, the husband must maintain a very connected relationship with

God. This is important because the husband is the spiritual head of the household. When he shows he takes this responsibility seriously, it provides an atmosphere that fosters a very connected relationship. Children are three times more likely to stay in church if it is the father who initiates church attendance, according to the Lifeway Research group.

Physical security comes in two stages. The **first stage** of physical security is that your wife feels no physical threat from you, her husband. Sadly, because of the high incidence of domestic abuse, we need to make the point that there will never be physical security if your wife feels you will ever raise your hand against her.

The **second stage** in physical security is for your wife to know that in every situation, you will protect her at all costs from any outside threat. The feeling of physical protection brings calmness like no other. You can do this in even slight gestures that show you are looking out for her. For instance, Melisa never wants to sleep on the side of the bed nearest the door. Her thoughts are that if anyone comes into our bedroom, she wants them to have to go through me (Steven) first.

There was also a time when I was not as diligent about checking the garage door at night to make sure it was locked. This caused some insecurity in Melisa related to the safety of our vehicles, her and our daughter. Because security is not a major issue, it did not even get on my radar. As I became aware, it was an issue for her it was an opportunity for me to step up and meet a need and give her value.

Finally, **financial security** is often looked at as being materialistic, but it is a very real need and one that needs to be taken seriously. **1 Timothy 5:8** tells us, *"But if anyone does not provide for his own, and especially for those of his household, he has denied the faith, and is worse than an unbeliever."*

You don't have to be a millionaire to provide financial security. What needs to be communicated is you are doing everything possible to meet the financial needs of the household. This may mean you are diligent with your budget, you are consistently working, and you are not frivolous with your spending.

If you have been dealt a blow and lost your job, she needs to know you are working tirelessly to gain employment to provide for her. We see many couples where the wife has a larger income than her husband. This does not mean you are not creating financial security. This is where stewardship and wisdom can increase her security, even if you are not providing the lion's share of the income. Knowing you will ensure she always has a home, food, and her basic needs will go a long way in confirming her need for financial security will be met.

The second most important need of a woman is Affection

Affection often means quite different things to men and women. They define affection in the dictionary as a tender feeling towards one another. Often, this can also be identified as non-sexual touch. Affection can also express care. It symbolizes protection, comfort, and approval.

When spouses are affectionate towards one another, it sends the following messages: "You are important to me, and I will care for and protect you." "I am concerned about the problems you face and will be there for you when you need me." Affection comes naturally during the dating process. However, affection becomes more important in marriage because it says you are still valuable and worth being pursued.

It is always better to be over-affectionate than under-affectionate. In doing this, you will eliminate any doubt about your feelings. Frequent simple gestures of kindness and physical touch are great ways to meet the need for affection. Holding hands, sitting with your arm around her, a kiss, or just the act of a gentle touch with no need for this to lead to sex are all important in making sure her need for affection is fully satisfied.

Such things as a kind word, a greeting card, a text message, or a love note unexpectedly tucked into her purse are always great ways to show affection. The goal is to make certain she always knows she is on your mind.

I (Melisa) have found that Steven has an amazing ability to be extremely affectionate. Personally, there are times I can become a little claustrophobic when people are in my personal space too often. Steven had to learn the balance of meeting my need for affection versus overwhelming me with his affection. This is where the art of becoming a student of your spouse will pay off big. If your spouse doesn't respond to a lot of physical touching, there are still many ways to communicate affection.

You can never go wrong if you ask your wife, "What kind of affection makes you feel the most loved?" This may seem like it shouldn't have to be done, but it is better to ask and get it right than to guess and get it wrong. Wives, if your husband asks something like this, don't treat him as if he should already know. Recognize he is just trying to get it right and wants you to feel the genuine affection he has in his heart for you. This is an opportunity to help him give you exactly what you want most.

The third need of a woman is
Open Communication

Conversation, not in generalities, but with details and emotion attached, is important. If, for instance, a friend is going to have a baby, the big day comes, and the father calls to tell you the good news. What are the questions your wife is going to ask you? How big is the baby? What gender is it? What is its name? When are they coming home from the hospital? Does it have a 'little putting green' tuft of hair, or is he/she bald? The list can be endless. The value and quality of the communication are relayed by using and including details.

Men, you may need to make a concerted effort to meet your wives' needs in this area. Women are freer to express emotion and details when communicating with others. Men communicate precisely and matter-of-factly. Studies show women use between 17,000 and 20,000 words a day, while men use only between 7,000 and 9,000; this may vary from person to person, but generally, this is true. My advice to you as a husband is to always save at least 500 words for your wife when you get home.

Most men are going to need to develop their communication skills to meet this need of their wives. It is only in some areas where they struggle. For example, when a man is telling another man about a car, he can communicate the make, model, horsepower, engine size, and details without difficulty. Husbands need to use that same type of communication to meet the communication needs of their wives. He does this both by listening to her and by mapping out the details of his heart.

Husbands, if you feel your wife is bombarding you with questions, this is a good indicator you are not meeting her communication needs. By providing conversation in sentences, not one-word answers, you will find the barrage of questions may subside. You can take the fear out of hearing her say, "We need to talk" by committing to a conversation. By being an active participant in a conversation, even starting them, you are building your marriage, meeting her needs, and drawing closer together.

Just a side note: if you haven't been providing open communication with your wife for a while, you may find, when you first commit to opening those lines, your wife will hit you with a deluge of talking. The more she feels this is going to be a life-long practice, she will eventually level out and her communication will be less overwhelming. Also, if communication in the past has been met with grumpiness, anger, or major shutdowns, I may also take a while for her to open up to you. Either way, give her the space and time to recognize that open communication is a need that you are more than HAPPY to meet!

Remember, body language is a huge part of communication. Talking to her while acting like you are going to the dentist is not relaying that you feel it is important to her. Turn off the tv, put away your phone, and attempt to turn and look her in the eyes. It conveys you are not doing it because you have to. A gift not freely given is not a gift. Give her the gift of communication and she will treasure it.

The fourth primary need of women is Leadership

Christ is the ultimate example of leadership. Look at how he invited the disciples to join him. We don't have an account of all 12, but we have several. In **Matthew 4:18-22,** Jesus invited Peter and Andrew by first helping them catch more fish. Leaders are to bring something to the table and then present to their followers some intriguing proposition like Jesus did when He said, *"I will make you fishers of men."* (**Mark 2:14**)

Even you, as the leader of your household, need to give your family a reason to believe. Here are two examples: Jesus boldly invited Matthew, a tax collector who was among the most reviled members of society, saying to him, "Follow Me." And then there was the calling of Nathanael. Nathaniel was very skeptical. "Can anything good come from Nazareth?" speaking of Jesus and his hometown. Jesus told Nathaniel something he had no business knowing, and it created a convert. See **John 1:43-51**.

Finally, leadership is not domination. One facet of leadership is getting others to willingly follow. Men are called to be the leaders of the home in many areas. Spiritual leadership is the most important area. Spiritual leadership involves Bible reading and Bible study, prayer, and getting involved in your church. Example provides leadership more than by using a verbal directive.

Leadership should also be demonstrated in the areas of finances, romance, and children. Wives need to provide an environment where men can remain in the leadership role God has designed for them. Women need to submit to the leadership of their husbands. Submission doesn't mean wives don't have a voice, just as it doesn't mean the husband is the boss. Submission is a gift of following your husband as he follows Christ.

This can be difficult if a woman comes from a home where her father did not assume his leadership role or where a mother dominated the relationship. This will be an area where women with powerful personalities may struggle. The benefit of strong leadership will be a clearly defined purpose and direction. This will enable the couple to work together as a unit and accomplish more in their relationship.

When wives will allow their husbands the opportunity to assume their role as leaders, they will see God's blessing on their marriage in amazing ways. Husbands, remember, if you are leading and no one is following you, you're just out for a walk. It may be time to adjust your leadership style.

Christ is the undisputed leader of the church, and the Bible specifically directs husbands to follow his example of leadership. Paul clearly lays out the concept that the husband is the head of the home in **Ephesians 5:23**, *"For the husband is the head of the wife as Christ is the head of the church, His body, of which He is the Savior."*

To replicate Christ's leadership in the marriage, let's look at who Christ leads and how Christ leads. Christ led his disciples and in a defining moment of His ability to lead, he served them by washing their feet. We find this story in **John 13:1-17**:

It was just before the Passover Festival. Jesus knew the hour had come for Him to leave this world and go to the Father. having loved His own who were in the world, He loved them to the end. The evening meal was in progress, and the devil had already prompted Judas, the son of Simon Iscariot, to betray Jesus.

Jesus knew the Father had put all things under His power, and that he had come from God and was returning to God; so He

47

got up from the meal, took off His outer clothing, and wrapped a towel around His waist. After that, He poured water into a basin and washed His disciples' feet, drying them with the towel that was wrapped around Him.

Jesus came to Simon Peter and said to Him, "Lord, are You going to wash my feet?"

Jesus replied, "You do not realize now what I am doing, but later you will understand."

"No," said Peter, "you shall never wash my feet."

Jesus answered, "Unless I wash you, you have no part with Me."

"Then, Lord," Simon Peter replied, "not just my feet, but my hands and my head as well!"

Jesus answered, "Those who have had a bath need only to wash their feet; their whole body is clean. And you are clean, though not every one of you." For He knew who was going to betray Him. That was why Jesus said not every one was clean.

When He had finished washing their feet, Jesus put on His clothes and returned to His place. "Do you understand what I have done for you?" He asked them. "You call me 'Teacher' and 'Lord,' and rightly so, for that is what I am. Now that I, your Lord and Teacher, have washed your feet, you also should wash one another's feet.

"I have set you an example that you should do as I have done for you. Very truly I tell you, no servant is greater than his master, nor is a messenger greater than the one who sent him.

Now that you know these things, you will be blessed if you do them."

In the middle of this encounter, Peter tries to refuse Christ's service and, as the ultimate servant/leader, Jesus convinces Peter that His service here, as shown by washing feet, is necessary. For great leadership to exist, great service needs to be present.

In **Philippians 2:7,** the Apostle Paul wrote this about Jesus: *"He made Himself nothing by taking the very nature of a servant, being made in human likeness."* Christ's surrendering heaven to become a man provides the ultimate example of sacrificial love, an essential component of marital leadership.

The art of having people follow you out of love will always involve some self-sacrifice. When you were dating, how often did you ask her to pay? It was easy to sacrifice your money and your free time all for her. You should always remember a husband's willingness to sacrifice himself for his wife and his family will encourage his wife's willingness to follow his leadership.

Chapter 5

Conflict Resolution

Marriage without conflict is not possible. The Bible says in **1 Corinthians 7:28**, *"He who marries will have trouble in this life."* While this is not a scripture you hear quoted at many weddings, it is an accurate statement. Conflict, however, doesn't mean anger. Conflict in a relationship is something that can help spur growth in the individuals involved if they properly handle it. It can also be something that wounds and causes damage to the heart of one or both of the people who are involved.

In conflict resolution, you can look at it as either a tug of war or as a give-and-take scenario. One way is confrontational and results in a winner and a loser. Another way is based on a compromise where both sides get something out of it. There are many ways to deal with conflict when it arises in marriage. Often, the way we deal with conflict is like the way we saw conflict handled by our family/parents or completely the opposite.

I (Melisa) was raised in a home where my mother and father had little conflicts. This was primarily because my mother avoided conflict. Her motto was, "It takes two people to fight." If one of them isn't fighting, then the other one will quickly run out of steam. She didn't see being right as something very important and therefore she was quite willing to adapt to whatever my father wanted. She did, however, on a rare occasion, hold her ground if she thought there was something particularly important at stake.

Because she so rarely took a stand, my father was quick to get into agreement with her when she did, so I came from a family where there was not a lot of conflict between my parents. This didn't mean I didn't have conflicts with my dad. I did, and often it was very unproductive for me. I learned conflict rarely ended the way I wanted it to, so it had little appeal for me.

In my first marriage, I learned increased decibels always accompanied conflict. Flying objects and harsh words also occasionally accompanied those increased decibels. This reinforced my belief that conflict was HIGHLY overrated, and I learned to avoid this at all costs.

I (Steven) grew up in a house where conflict was a battle of wits. Almost no one ever yelled or screamed, but you knew you had crossed someone when the insults started flying, and then it was on. It rarely resulted in one side surrendering, and it usually resulted in somebody getting his or her feelings hurt. This is usually the case when every altercation involves proving you are better, smarter, or more correct.

When we got together, the birds chirped, the angels sang, and there was peace all around for a while. Steven's mother was genuinely concerned that we had not fought prior to our wedding. However, to reassure her, we had our first fight the night before our wedding, and it was a doozy. Probably because we were both tired and a significant conflict between Steven and his brother had primed the pump, we were ripe for an argument.

I (Melisa) had gotten Steven a new cross necklace for a wedding gift. As we sat on the floor of our bedroom, it thrilled me to present him with this token of my great love for him. He opened it, looked at it, and said thanks. I thought my heartfelt choosing of the perfect wedding gift would net me copious amounts of praise, and all I got was "Thank you." My feelings were trampled on, and the crying started.

Steven was angry because he thought, "Thank you," was an appropriate response, and that was where expectations and emotions collided. I got my feelings hurt, Steve got defensive, and we got introduced to arguing for the first time. The honeymoon was officially over, and we hadn't even gotten married yet.

With the enormity of the next day's events, we quickly got over ourselves and had a wonderful, beautiful wedding. Getting over yourself leads us to our next point.

Frequently, selfishness causes conflict. We often find ourselves in conflict because we have the desire to have the other person do what we want them to do. The attitude where you feel it's necessary to get your way invites the spirit of division into the relationship. When we can stop ourselves in the middle of a conversation and try to determine if selfishness is driving the conflict, we are better able to reframe our expectations and see resolutions that will be beneficial to both parties.

Philippians 2:3-4 is a fitting example of how to treat other people.

"Do nothing from selfishness or empty conceit, but with humility of mind, regard one another as more important than yourselves; do not merely look out for your own personal interests, but also for the interests of others."

Luke 9:23 reminds us, *"Then Jesus said to them all, "Whoever wants to be My disciple must deny himself, take up his cross daily, and follow Me."* This scripture gives us a framework for how to view ourselves. When you combine these two Biblical blueprints, it allows you to uproot selfishness and gives you the upper hand in creating a peaceful solution to your conflicts.

When we empty ourselves of selfishness and allow God to fill us up with love, we find conflict resolution comes much quicker. Here is a great list of what love is and what love isn't:

"Love is patient, love is kind and is not jealous; love does not brag and is not arrogant, does not act unbecomingly; it does not seek its own, is not provoked, does not consider a wrong suffered,

does not rejoice in unrighteousness, but rejoices with the truth; bears all things, believes all things, hopes all things, endures all things. Love never fails." (**1 Corinthians 13:4-8**)

We often read this passage at weddings, and for good reason. As we read this passage, we see the very definition of love. Walking in love is the key to successful conflict resolution. When in conflict, both parties may provide input, but they must do so lovingly and respectfully. Love can accomplish more towards ending a fight than any cleverly constructed argument can.

Forgiveness is vital to conflict resolution. Resolving conflict doesn't happen if one or both people involved are unwilling to forgive. Withholding forgiveness is the acid that eats away at a successful long-term resolution. Forgiveness neutralizes the acidity in the relationship and promotes long-term stability. At the end of a conflict, you must come to a place where any forgiveness needed has been provided. This is crucial to having conflict resolution.

Forgiveness also means there is no score keeping. 1 Corinthians 13:5 reminds us love takes no account of wrongs done to it. "(Love) *does not consider* (or *keep track of) a wrong suffered."* When one or both people become historical (and/or hysterical) during the conflict, a resolution is very delayed or not possible. By choosing to forgive, you bring the conflict to a place where resolution is possible.

Matthew 6:14-15 says, *"If you forgive others for their transgressions, your heavenly Father will also forgive you. But if you do not forgive others, then your Father will not forgive your transgressions."* Not only does forgiveness help you in the sweet by and by, but it provides immeasurable benefits in the nasty here and now. If it helps you now and it helps you later, there is no reason not to incorporate it immediately so you can start reaping the benefits immediately.

There are several ways to prevent or quickly resolve conflict in a marriage. These simple techniques, when used, invite the spirit of unity and bring glory to God.

The first technique is to
Be Quiet

Try not to counter an idea before you have allowed it to be fully presented. When you listen intentionally to what your spouse is saying and allow them to fully present their position without thinking about what your response will while they are talking, it will help prevent you from jumping to unnecessary or inaccurate conclusions.

James 1:19-20 tells us, *"My dear brothers and sisters, take note of this: Everyone should be quick to listen, slow to speak and slow to become angry because human anger does not produce the righteousness that God desires."* This may be difficult for some, but is a habit worth forming.

Proverbs 15:18 says, *"A hot-tempered man stirs up dissension, but a patient man calms a quarrel."* By not allowing your spouse to fully present their position and by interrupting them, you often create unnecessary arguments. Remember, if you cannot or will not listen fully to the other person's position, the fight isn't over and there is still unresolved conflict. Remember, you are a team and a win for one is a win for both. Do your part to make sure you are a good team player and you are working to bring about a win-win resolution.

The second technique is to
Be Still

This is like being quiet, but it is not the same thing. Being still allows you time to consider the other side. It also gives the Lord the opportunity to speak to your situation. **Psalm 46:10** says, *"Be still and know I am God."*

We find another example of the benefits of being still in **1 Kings 19:11-13**:

"Then He said, "Go out, and stand on the mountain before the Lord." And behold, the Lord passed by, and a great and strong wind tore into the mountains and broke the rocks into pieces before the Lord, but the Lord was not in the wind. And after the wind there was an earthquake, but the Lord was not in the earthquake. After the earthquake a fire, but the Lord was not

in the fire. And after the fire, there was a still, small voice. That was when Elijah heard His voice."

God wants you to be still so you can hear his voice. God is a gentleman and won't interrupt. When you take time to be still, you allow the Holy Spirit to infuse discernment into what you are about to say. This will promote peace and prevent hurt feelings from harmful and injuring words.

Proverbs 15:1 says, *"A quiet answer deflects anger, but harsh words make tempers flare."* When you are still and respond quietly and peacefully, you invite a peaceful resolution. One thing to recognize is that being still is not a license to isolate your spouse. There is a difference between taking time to consider the other person's position and providing a measured, loving, and respectful response versus giving the other person the cold shoulder or putting them in the penalty box.

Withholding communication is not conflict resolution. It just delays dealing with a conflict. Sometimes in conflict when you need to get quiet alone. If you recognize tempers are flaring and the intensity of the conflict is rising, calling a time-out for a designated period allows everyone to calm down and seek God for the solution to the problem. It is very difficult, if not impossible, to hear God when your emotions are high. Just remember, if you call a timeout in the middle of a conflict, you must go back and revisit it in a timely fashion for a resolution to be reached.

The third technique is to always
Be Aware of Tone and Body Language

Seventy percent of communication is nonverbal. Often, we see people are disrespectful when they are angry. They speak in a disrespectful tone or use disrespectful words. Disrespect doesn't have to be loud or angry, but they can deliver it in a matter-of-fact tone with malicious intentions by using sarcasm.

I (Steven) grew up in a house where we never raised our voices to each other but engaged routinely in bouts of verbal one-upmanship with sarcasm as our primary weapon. Having been raised with sarcasm, it was mother's milk to me, and just like mother's milk, I needed to be weaned off it.

You can choose your words to inflict the most damage or to do the most good. But either way, it is still a choice. You can undo a lot of flowery words if your tone and body language show they are insincere. An icy apology through gritted teeth communicates the opposite of "I'm sorry." Not only aren't you sorry, but a clenched jaw shows you are unwilling to budge from your position.

Making sure your body language, words, and tone of voice, all communicate respect, will prevent unnecessary hurt and an escalation of the conflict. Choosing to act and speak respectfully invites peace and resolution and allows the other person to feel heard and understood.

The fourth technique is to
Use Points of Agreement

Using statements that acknowledge you have heard the other person and validate their position brings about a quicker resolution from a calmer place. Acknowledging statements might include: "I see where you're coming from." "That's a good point." "I can see that." "I can understand where you got that from, from what I said." These are just a few of the statements that show you are still actively listening to the other person. It also shows your willingness to see their point of view.

You always want to make sure your acknowledging statements are sincere and from the heart, so they promote peace. If they come across as condescending, they will more likely just pour gas on the fire of an already volatile conversation. Points of agreement may not end an argument, but they can take the wind out of the sails. This has the effect of preventing escalation. It is also an excellent reminder that the two of you are on the same team. A sight often lost in the middle of an argument.

The fifth technique is to
Ask Clarifying Questions

Unfortunately, we don't all come into conversations or conflicts from the same perspective. Asking clarifying questions such as, "Can you help with that?" or "Can you tell me more about it?" will let the other person know he has been heard, and it allows you to get more information on the table so both sides can find a resolution easier. Much like stillness and quietness work together, acknowledging statements and clarifying questions work together. Clarifying questions transmits value by saying to the other person, "I want to understand you correctly."

Giving value at the beginning of the conflict helps promote security and safety, which leads to calm solutions. Hopefully, clarifying questions are received as your partner wanting to 'get it right' and not as being petty or annoying. There have been situations in the middle of a fight where Melisa has let me know with vigor that she is only asking a clarifying question. That is the point where I have to throw my hands up in surrender. She has used our tools to her advantage. It forced me to slow down, cool off, and consider what she was asking.

Remember, in any conflict, the goal is not victory but resolution

Before you begin a conflict, you must take some time and think through what a resolution for that situation would look like. What do you need out of the conversation? Do you need to be heard? Do you need something to change?

Ask yourself what you are willing to bring to the situation to make it a win-win and help both of you have a resolution. Never end a conflict without asking each other, "Have we come to a resolution? Are we okay?" If one of you doesn't feel like the conflict has been resolved, discuss what you need in order to do so. Stay in the conversation until you have resolved things between the two of you. Doing this will ensure you don't keep having the same conflict over and over. The goal in a conflict is to always end it WITH a resolution!

Chapter 6

The Greatest Wedding Present Ever

Keeping in mind, we are building around the idea of a God-centered marriage. When we look at sex, let's look at what God says about it. One thing we want to do is to reframe how people think about sex and the Bible, God's guidebook for everything, including sex. So, to do that, let's look at what the Bible says about stripper poles. Take a moment and give that some thought. If you came up with nothing, you are absolutely right. About the only thing you can take away from that is, if you have one, you'd better be married to the one using the pole and it should be in your home.

There are many misconceptions about what God says about sex in the Bible, and we hope to dispel them in this chapter. It is God Who created sex. It gets better than that. Everything He creates is good, and He gave it to us. By us, I mean married couples. You can primarily find the "Do's and Don'ts of Sex" in a couple of places. You find a lot of the Don'ts in **Leviticus, chapter 18**. Don't throw it out just because it's the Old Testament. It's in the Bible for a reason.

Before you get too wound up about the 47 Biblical rules you're about to get that'll suck the joy out of your sex life, let's take a closer look. What the Bible speaks against are things that society, and not just Christians, frown upon; things like don't sleep with your mom or stepmom, brothers and sisters, nieces and nephews, brother- and sisters-in-law, neighbors, same-sex partners, and no animals. There is no call for a lot of outside-the-box thinking here. It leaves an awful lot that is allowable. Therefore, sex is one of God's most wonderful gifts.

God does nothing without a purpose and sex is no different. What was the Lord thinking when He came up with such an outstanding idea?

The first reason behind sex is to forge a covenant between a man and a woman.

"For this reason, a man will leave his father and mother and be united to his wife, and the two shall become one flesh." (**Genesis 2:24**) A covenant is about surrendering your rights and assuming your responsibilities. The world is all about the marriage contract. Contracts have the reverse effect. They are about protecting your rights and limiting your responsibilities.

The increasing use of prenuptial contracts displays this. Nowadays, you don't even have to be ultra-wealthy to go into a marriage looking to "protect what's yours." That attitude already limits your ability to become one flesh because you are withholding from each other. Sex for a married couple is the only activity 100% exclusive to a husband and wife.

You will eventually do almost everything else with someone else. Praying, laughing, eating, working, and going to church are all great and all are better with other people. Sex is like the great toy you got for Christmas and didn't want to share with your brothers and sisters. The best thing about it is you do not have to share it and you should not share it.

The next reason God created sex is for Procreation

The bonus round of great sex is you get to have kids, and eventually grandkids. We have ten, and they are the best! You never get the joys of grand-parenting without first having kids. There is nothing better than a happy baby face. As proud grandparents, we can attest to that. Children are an amazing blessing. God allows us to double dip in the pleasure department with sex and kids. The directive is simple and spelled out in **Genesis 1:27-28**. *"So God created mankind in His Own image. He created both a male and a female. God blessed them and said to them, "Be fruitful and increase in number to fill the* *earth and subdue it.*" It's simple, straightforward, and from the Lord.

The third reason, saving the best for last, is for Pleasure

Yes, I said it. God wants us to have great, satisfying, and pleasure-filled sex on into our golden years. How do we know this? All you must do is go to the **Song of Solomon**. From its opening verses in **chapter 1, verse 2**: "*Let him kiss me with the kisses of his mouth for your love is more delightful than any wine,*" and then on to **verse 4** "*Take me away with you – let us hurry! Let the king bring me to his chamber.*"

Let us not skip the final in **Chapter 8, verse 14**: "*Come away, my lover, and be like a gazelle or like a young stag on the spice-laden mountains.*"

Throughout the entire book's eight chapters, Solomon paints a picture of passion, beauty, and, yes, sex from courtship through marriage to the honeymoon bed, as God intended it. Sometimes it's more symbolic speaking of gazelles, spices, and fruits... and at other times, it takes no imagination when talking about kissing or saying, "He is my lover."

The original intent of God was for a husband and wife to live together without shame. When God created Adam and Eve in the garden, there was no sense of shame. **Genesis**

1:25. However, we note that, after introducing sin into their lives, shame followed.

The author detailed this in **Genesis 3:7-10**:

Both of them had their eyes opened, and they realized they were naked; so they sewed fig leaves together and made coverings for themselves. Then the man and his wife heard the Lord God as He was walking in the garden in the cool of the day, and they hid from the Lord God among the trees of the garden. But the Lord God called to the man, 'Where are you?"

Adam answered, "I heard You in the garden, and I was afraid because I was naked. So, I hid."

It is interesting to notice here that they sewed fig leaves to cover their genitals. This was the original indicator of the entrance of shame. One of the best ways to avoid attaching shame to sex in your marriage is to always be diligent to treat your spouse respectfully. Respect is the antidote to shame. There are several ways to show respect for your spouse regarding sex.

Some of the best ways to show respect are:

Respect your spouse's boundaries

Creativity in the bedroom is wonderful. It generates excitement and expectation, all the while preventing boredom. However, when any area of creativity causes your spouse to feel uncomfortable or shamed, it is important to be sensitive to this. It is NOT okay to cross any boundary your spouse has.

They also need to feel completely okay saying no with no repercussions. "No" means no.

Respect each person's sexual history

Our history involves more than just how many previous partners we've had. The attitude towards sex we were raised with contributes to our history as well. A person's sexual history should never be used as a weapon against them. This includes the tendency to compare them to previous partners. Prior sexual sins are just that, prior. What is in the past shouldn't be dredged up to put your spouse in a negative or shameful light. If your spouse has repented, that is good enough for God and it should be good enough for you. We don't dwell on the past. We learn from it.

Respect your spouse's desire for sex

We want to remind you that sex is God's idea, His gift, and His creation. You should never make your spouse feel guilty for wanting sex. God built a sex drive into all of us, just in varying degrees. If your husband/wife wants sex more or less, you need to respect that for each other.

Being able to talk openly and honestly about sex is vital. Open communication will reduce the opportunity for shame to attach itself to sex during marriage. It will allow a husband and wife to embrace it without fear. Sometimes, it will be a novel experience for one or both of you. It's an exciting path you can walk down together. You need to establish solid communication about sex to prevent hurt and resentment and shame from taking up residence in your marriage bed.

Speaking of the marriage bed, scripture specifically deals with purity inside marriage. **Hebrews 13:4** states, "*Marriage should be honored by all, and the marriage bed kept pure, for God will judge the adulterer and all the sexually immoral.*"

It sounds so simple looking at it from the early stage of marriage. Keep in mind the words of Jesus in **Matthew 5:28**: "*But I tell you that anyone who looks at a woman lustfully has already committed adultery with her in his heart.*"

You are going to have a fulfilling sex life when you can honor the marriage bed in both thought and deed. Not that we must walk through life staring at the ground for fear of seeing an attractive member of the opposite sex and violating Christ's directions. It is to remind us to be mentally disciplined enough not to dwell on or fantasize about what we see as we protect the sanctity of our marriage beds.

This gets harder and harder to do with the bombardment of sexual images and the rampant availability of pornography in society today. A common misconception about pornography is it is not adultery because there is no physical interaction and no one gets hurt because there is no violence. This couldn't be further from the truth. The words of Christ dispel the ideas about adultery. The violence is emotional, and the hurt is very real and deep for the spouse of the pornography user.

Many times, people who engage in the ongoing use of pornography develop a distorted sense of sexual priorities. Pornography becomes their most important sexual relationship, overtaking their sexual relationship with their spouse. For many, they developed the relationship with pornography in adolescence and continue into adulthood. This long-term relationship causes a pattern of destruction that repeats itself if the relationship is to remain intact.

The relationship with pornography must end completely. Stopping from using it first requires going to God with a repentant heart. No long-term solution will remain in place on man's strength alone. By white-knuckling it, you are setting yourself up for failure. There is a warning in **Proverbs 26:11**, *"Like a dog returning to his vomit so is a fool who repeats his folly."*

Many times, the shame of using pornography prevents people from seeking help. To repeat patterns that have been unsuccessful in the past is to live out the warning in **Proverbs 26**.

Another saying is, "Repeating the same behavior while expecting different results is the definition of insanity. After going to God, you must be brave enough to seek spiritual guidance and accountability from people who have had success in this area. Involving others in the healing process reduces the powerful hold that secrets can have. Secrets in a marriage make it sick, especially if those secrets start in the bedroom.

Two scriptures speak specifically to this idea.

- *"Therefore confess your sins one to another and pray for each other that you may be healed. The prayer of a righteous man is powerful and effective."* (**James 5:16**)

and also...

- *"For you were once in darkness, but now you are in the light of the Lord. Live as children of the light (for the fruit of the light consists in all goodness, righteousness, and truth) and find out what pleases the Lord. Have nothing to do with the fruitless deeds of darkness, but rather expose them. For it is shameful even to mention what the disobedient do in secret. But everything exposed by the light becomes visible for the light makes everything visible."* (**Ephesians 5:8-14**)

By releasing the powerful hold of this secret, you will bring healing and restoration to your sexual relationship with your spouse.

How do you address your spouse in the bedroom? There are two sets of needs that should always be addressed in healthy marital sex — your needs and the needs of the other. You can often become absorbed in your needs, wants, and desires. This can let selfishness creep in. In the Conflict Resolution chapter, selfishness is the root of many conflicts. Conflict in the bedroom can lead to only sleeping in the bedroom. There are very few marriages that can survive this. Selfish sex is ungodly sex.

God's design for sex is further laid out in **1 Corinthians 7:3-5**:

"The husband should fulfill his marital duty to his wife, and likewise, the wife to her husband. The wife does not have authority over her own body but yields it to her husband. In the same way, the husband does not have over his own body but yields it to his wife. Do not deprive each other except by mutual consent and for a time, so you may devote yourself to prayer. Then come together again so Satan will not tempt you because of your lack of self-control."

Sex is such a powerful tool in making great marriages. Satan will seek to turn it against marriages. How do we keep Satan out of our bedrooms? The same way we keep him out of everywhere else, with prayer. This is a revolutionary concept when it comes to sex. You don't keep God out of your kitchen or dining room. Many times, on a cold Minnesota day, I (Steve) have prayed that my car would start. There isn't a big red circle with a slash through it that prevents God from seeing what's going on in your bedroom or in any other area of your life.

Welcome God into your sex life. After all, it is his idea. Try praying before sex. It may sound funky, but give it a shot. Then afterward, you can thank him for the best wedding present ever. You'll find yielding too, and seeking God in your sex life will allow you to reap all the benefits found in the **Song of**

Solomon. It will also strengthen you in the areas where the enemy may try to attack your sexual integrity. From chapter one, we've talked about God being at the center of your marriage. You'll find everything is better when you involve God in it, especially sex.

Chapter 7

Money! Money! Money!

One of the most often misquoted Scripture passages is **1 Timothy 6:10**, often being quoted as, "Money is the root of all evil." The Scripture says, "It is the LOVE of money that is the root of all evil." In the society we live in today, we see the love of money almost everywhere we look. From professional athletes to the multi-millionaire business people like Donald Trump. It seems everyone in the United States is busy chasing the "almighty" dollar. Christians, mostly, are not much different in that aspect. While money is important and we need it to live, how we manage it in a marriage is more important.

Before you say the "I Do's," keeping your money separate is the best approach. However, after the ring is on the finger, it's time to join your assets. If they are "our" kids, and we live in "our" house, it should be "our" money. Because of the extremely high incidence of divorce in our country, we have seen an increase in prenuptial agreements and separate bank accounts. By joining your money, however, you are not starting the marriage with the idea that if this goes badly, I can just take MY money and leave.

There are many topics to cover in finances in marriage. Let's get first things first.

First, money is important

The Bible talks more about money than it does about faith. It can be the source of great blessings or the source of what some people would consider a curse.

The Bible is clear about the way to ensure that blessings flow into your life through money.

"I, the Lord, do not change. So, you, the descendants of Jacob, are not destroyed. Ever since the time of your ancestors, you have turned away from my decrees and have not kept them. Return to Me and I will return to you," says the Lord Almighty. "You ask, 'How are we to return?' Will a mere mortal rob God? Yet you rob Me."

"You also ask, 'How are we robbing You?'"

"In tithes and offerings. You are under a curse—your whole nation—because you are robbing Me. Bring the whole tithe into the storehouse, that there may be food in My house. Test Me in this," says the Lord Almighty, "and see Me throw open the flood-gates of heaven and pour out so much blessing that there will not

be room enough to store it. I will prevent pests from devouring your crops, and the vines in your fields will not drop their fruit before it is ripe," says the Lord Almighty. "Then all the nations will call you blessed, for your land will be delightful," says the Lord Almighty."

Malachi 3:6-12

Just like sex is a covenant between a husband and wife, tithing is a covenant between you and God. It is important to establish, prior to marriage, that tithing will be non-negotiable in your marriage. Tithing refers to giving God the first ten percent of your increase. This includes paychecks, sales, gifts, and any other way the money finds its way to you. By ensuring agreement on tithing, you are ensuring God will provide His blessing. The Bible is clear that not only will God provide an increase, but He will also rebuke the devourer for your sake. Therefore, tithing is paramount in finances. When you commit to tithing BEFORE you are married, you start your marriage off with the blessings of God in place.

When we first met online, we spent many hours talking on the phone. When I (Melisa) brought up tithing, Steven was really not interested in giving his money to the church. He thought it was better to give his time to the church as his tithe, and after all, he occasionally plunked $10 into the bucket. I told Steven that tithing wasn't optional and that it was how we showed obedience to God.

I will never forget the next statement he made. "Well, I will have to have a scriptural directive to do that." Oddly enough, I could rattle off several scriptures that talk about tithing, such as **Deuteronomy 26:12**; **Malachi 3:10**; and **Luke 20:22-25**. Being a man of his word, Steven saw the "scriptural directive" and began to tithe.

Offerings differ from tithes. Offerings are monies you give in addition to the tithe. These are great and should be done as God guides you to do so. It is important, however, to decide how much of an offering can be made without the agreement of your spouse. Setting a limit on the size of the offering to be given is a great way to ensure conflict will not arise.

Communication in marriage when it relates to finances is crucial. By starting your marriage with openness about where you are in your finances and committing to being transparent about spending, you will have better success in managing your finances and your marriage.

When we got serious about our relationship and knew that getting married was God's plan for our lives. I (Steven) decided Melisa should know exactly where I stood as far as my finances were concerned. On a trip to Oklahoma, I brought along a canvas book bag. Much to her dismay, this bag did not include a gift for her or any of her children, but it did include a big surprise.

Feeling compelled to be honest and open about my wealth, or lack of it, I revealed the contents of the bag to her. I dumped on her floor three and a half months' worth of credit card bills, phone bills, and gym membership bills, many of which weren't even opened and two-thirds of which weren't paid. I had never been good at math, so budgeting did not come easy. Rather than learn it, I ignored it and reaped what I sowed.

I (Melisa) must admit it shocked me to see his lack of money management. However, because we were still in the love-is-blind phase of our relationship; I was certain this would not be a problem. Luckily for me, Steven is a man of character and did what was best for his soon-to-be family. We organized the bills and developed a plan to deal with them. So, if you find yourself in this kind of situation, it is far better in the long run, to be honest, and open and correct any problems before you get married.

One of the best ways to develop transparency in spending is by utilizing a budget and a daily accounting of your spending. This allows everyone to know where the money is going and prevents the inclination to hide expenditures. Many have heard the idea about women buying clothes, purses, and shoes and then hiding them in the closet until a later date, only to say they have had them for "a long time."

This kind of deception in finances is very hazardous to your marriage. By understanding that when secrets are revealed, they have a devastating power; it is far better to not have them to start with. By starting the marriage with a clear budget and an agreement to stay within the budget, you will build long-term success in your finances. It is important to pray about major decisions, especially in spending. This allows God to be involved in the decision-making process and will many times prevent rash and impulsive spending.

Often in marriage, you will find one spouse is a spender, and one will be a saver. This can cause conflict if you do not identify ahead of time how your money will be spent. You may also find that one spouse is better at managing money (i.e., number crunching) than the other. This is a fun time to use the gifts that are available in your marriage.

While the husband is the head of the family, it doesn't mean he has to be the one who balances the checkbook and pays the bills if the wife is better at it. It does mean, however, that whoever pays the bills and balances the bank accounts needs to be open and willing to review these with their spouse.

It is important to discuss having spending money or an allowance for each person.

It is important in marriage to provide each spouse with a previously decided upon amount of money that is theirs to spend however they wish. This allows for each one to not feel like they must justify every purchase they make.

If the husband wants to buy games for his gaming system but the wife feels this is a waste of money, using his own spending money for games allows him to feel like he can have something he wants and prevents her from feeling like he is wasting the household budget money.

The same is true for women who enjoy shopping for

clothes, purses, jewelry, and shoes. The wife has the freedom to purchase the things she desires without having to feel guilty. This allows for the freedom to spend money, but it also allows the freedom to spend money without the feeling of judgment. There is no stupid use in individual spending money. Providing a judgment-free atmosphere allows your spouse to feel you love them, whatever their idiosyncrasies may be.

Dave Ramsey says, "Money is fun... if you have some." It is especially true in the next topic related to finances, debt. Debt can be one of the most destructive forces within marriage and is one of the primary reasons cited for divorce in this country. Especially early in your marriage, debt may be hard to avoid, and if you come into the marriage with debt, it will be something you have to learn to deal with.

Debt needs to be a houseguest who will eventually leave and not become a lifelong member of the family. If you are starting your marriage with no debt, then it will be easier to maintain a life without it. Learning to live within your means will be one of the best things you can do to ensure marital success.

I (Melisa) have a quote I learned many years ago from my spiritual father. He would always say, "When your outgo exceeds your income, your upkeep will become your downfall." This is a timeless truth worth heeding.

Many times, people get caught up in the trap of "keeping up with the Joneses." This causes many people to justify the idea of purchasing things by going into debt to get them. This concept, along with the idea many young people have that they should immediately start their marriage with the same standard of living their parents have achieved after working for many years, can be a very dangerous place to be.

Being willing to forgo a few luxuries until you can pay cash for them is not always fun, but it is a great way to decrease your financial burdens in the future. By not spending tomorrow's earnings today, you will find it set your marriage up for success. By decreasing your financial burdens, you decrease the burdens in your marriage, and therefore decrease the weight for everyone to bear.

God knows the destructive power debt has on people and He provides us with this knowledge through His word. **Proverbs 22:7** talks about *"the borrower being subject to the lender,"* and **Romans 13:8** says, *"We should owe no man anything but to love them."* The great thing about "owing no man anything but to love him" is that love doesn't charge interest and earns a great return on your investment.

One great lie about finances is the dependence on your credit and FICO scores. If you are choosing to live a life with debt, then your credit and FICO scores are important. However, if you choose to live a life free of debt and pay cash for what you buy, then these two numbers are much less relevant. The only way to build your credit score is to borrow money. This completely defeats the idea of paying cash for your purchases.

Debt brings with it interest, which causes you to pay more

for what you are buying than what it is actually worth. Saving to buy what you want is a way to make interest. Also, paying cash will frequently get you a better deal. By current standards, if you purchase a house with a mortgage, you will find you are paying more than twice the price for it with the interest you are required to pay.

If you purchase a new vehicle with credit, you are going to lose twenty percent of the value when you drive off the lot. You would never borrow money to purchase stocks that are guaranteed to lose 20% of their value.

The final topic to be addressed is stewardship

We can define stewardship as the responsible planning and use of resources. When you embrace the idea that God is the master of your life and everything you have belongs to Him, it makes becoming a good steward of your resources much easier. *"By wisdom, a house is built and through understanding, it is established; **through** knowledge, its rooms are filled with rare and beautiful treasures."* (**Proverbs 24:3-4**)

With proper stewardship of the resources God has provided us, we will ensure we can survive in both prosperous and difficult financial climates. A great Biblical example of stewardship is the story of Joseph. It's in the story of Joseph where we see the combination of knowledge, divine inspiration, and resources in a classic example of stewardship guiding

Egypt from prosperity through famine and back to prosperity (**Genesis 41**).

Stewardship is the final piece of the financial puzzle, and by employing the concepts previously discussed, you will see proper stewardship of your resources.

Chapter 8

Family is Funky (and Everybody Has One)

When you purchase a new deck of cards, all the suits are separated as well as the numbers being in order. This is a great representation of families before the wedding. Once the couple has joined into the covenant relationship of marriage, the deck gets shuffled. The merging of two families is exactly how God designed it. However, in this era, it can be one of the hardest things to do.

With families that are very mobile and less traditional, it can become a laborious task. Today, with the preponderance of blended families, sometimes it's like shuffling two or three decks at once. By simply developing a plan prior to the wedding, you can avoid traps that many couples find themselves in.

A top priority in the successfully joining two families starts with each person being very intentional about building a relationship with their spouse's family. This is the first key in the successful shuffling of the cards. It requires both spouses to work together to help identify the unique characteristics of their own family. Each of you must become a student of your spouse's family. While learning something new is difficult, you have a wonderful gift in your spouse. You have a tutor that has many years of experience with the family which you are learning about. By working together, this process can be smooth and pleasant.

Some of the important details that should be learned include family expectations of time spent together, holiday traditions, religious beliefs and practices, and other unique family expectations. Today's society, where more and more people are in their second and third marriages, may make this more difficult. It will, however, also allow for a wider variety of experiences and traditions to be drawn from.

While it is not always possible to accommodate all the traditions of both families, talking about those traditions with each other, developing a plan, and presenting that plan to your families before the wedding will eliminate a significant amount of stress and hurt feelings after the wedding. Because in most cases every family wants to have some input into the wedding, this is a great opportunity to expand the conversation to future family traditions and expectations, allowing you to honor both families' traditions while establishing new traditions for your own family.

I (Melisa) was raised in a very conservative home. My

parents were nearly teetotalers. I, having grown up in a Southern Baptist church, thought people who drank were not in a relationship with Christ. Yes, I get that this is very Pharisaical, but that was what I believed. I spent most of my life living by this religious code. Then I met Steven and the Zimmermans. Steven was raised in a "nearly" Catholic family. They didn't subscribe to my overzealous ban on alcohol. Football was a family tradition in both of our houses. They celebrated it differently at Steven's.

The first time I met Steven's family was on a football Sunday. It was a very regular occurrence for his family to gather at his mother's house and watch the Minnesota Vikings play football. They have a unique tradition of toast touchdowns. These toasts included everyone, from the oldest to the youngest. While the minor children toasted with cranberry juice, they did so with their special shot glasses.

My first impression of this celebration was shock and awe. It took a while for me to realize this behavior wasn't criminal. It's not an activity we adopted in our house, but I've learned to honor it as a tradition at my in-laws.

As a couple, it is vital to decide regarding your plans for serving God. You must decide where to attend church and how you will be involved in serving at your church. This is a decision that only the two of you must make. It will, though, have the potential to affect both families in a big way. This decision must be discussed and agreed upon before presenting it to your families. For some, this may bring with it more pressure than for others.

If your families both have the same religious beliefs, this will be simpler than if they have very different beliefs. The sanctity of this decision is like the sanctity of the marriage, it is for the wedding couple alone. While our family is a great voice of counsel, it is not the replacement for the voice of God. It is through the leading of the Holy Spirit that provides the direction for your place of worship and service. Your decision should be presented to the family respectfully. You should not let your decision on how and where to serve God be unduly influenced by your families.

Holiday traditions, too, can be a source of great conflict. Many families have very specific traditions that they want to continue. By discussing and developing a plan for those traditions before the wedding, you will find there may be ways to accommodate both families. It is important to remember when you are discussing family traditions that each family may have very strong emotional ties to their tradition.

It is important to avoid using phrases such as "my family always" or "my family never," as this may promote defensiveness and close the door to compromise. A new member of our family reminded us that her family always goes Black Friday shopping. This conflicted with our plans. Eventually, technology saved the day, and online shopping eliminated the issue. There was going to be the need for a compromise if it hadn't.

When looking at this idea, it is important to honor the traditions of both families, but leave enough flexibility to establish traditions of your own. One of the most successful new traditions we've established is Friday Giving. Our family grew to where our kids, between their houses, our house, and the in-laws' houses, were driving around like crazy, and overfeeding their kid's turkey and stuffing.

We created un-Thanksgiving at our house on the following Friday with a menu of Mexican, Asian, fish fry, crab boil, and anything but turkey. There is now no hurry on Thanksgiving Day. There were no other meals to get to. A leisurely meal and family time have become valued and enjoyed by all.

Another creative way I (Melisa) instilled a greater sense of family is through Christmas ornaments. I buy a new ornament every year for every grandchild. It has gotten so big that the grandkids have their own tree. The kids go to the tree every year to find their new ornament. A word-to-the-wise: consider how many grandkids you will have when starting something like this.

Family baggage and history are something every couple must deal with as their marriage begins. This is something you both need to be aware of, so you are not always stepping on the toes of other members of your family. For instance: is one parent an alcoholic, is anyone in the family a vegetarian, or does someone in the family have a significant pet allergy?

These are all the things that need to be identified, and a developed plan on how to deal with them. If this can be done prior to the wedding, you can then start with everyone on the same page. This goes back to being a student of your spouse's family. Take time to get past the cliff notes and get an in-depth working knowledge of the people who will be a part of your family for the rest of your life.

A key area for significant discussion is when there are ex-spouses to accommodate. If you are blending a family, you must establish parameters for dealing with the other biological parents of your children. Taking into consideration the feelings of children, and honoring their parent's role in family traditions in the same way you would wish to be honored, will promote harmony and unity, even in the most difficult of family situations.

One of the essential elements to bridging the gaps between the two families was when I (Steve) started praying for the kid's birth dad. Mark was always a part of the kid's life. It was easier for some kids if we stayed separate. Praying helped them see we weren't enemies.

We got to the place where he came over with his dog and fixed our lawnmower, and our dogs and his dog had a playdate. Everyone attended most of the family functions in the latter stages of his life. This is a perfect cause for celebration!

Deciding whether to have children is another critical decision. If you have a child, it's a choice that you can't reverse. Having an agreement on this topic before the wedding is of paramount importance. While you can't always plan the timing of when to have children, discussing the desire to have, or not to have, children preceding the wedding will set up the two of you for success.

Having children will change the path of your married life forever and alter the definition of family. This single event will change the dynamics of your relationship more than any other event. It can bring with it incredible amounts of joy, but can also be accompanied by an incredible amount of stress.

You can never fully grasp how the addition of children will affect your life. However, you can move into an agreement on many things concerning your family by allowing for significant discussion before the marriage.

Children are indeed a blessing from the Lord. *"Behold, children are a heritage from the Lord. The fruit of the womb, a reward like arrows in the hand of a warrior are the children of one's youth. Blessed is the man who fills his quiver with them."* **(Psalm 127:3-4)**

Our sons have taken that scripture seriously. Mark has four kids and Levon has five. Children, while they will affect the relationship between a husband and wife, should never come before your relationship with your spouse. God created the husband and wife to be equals.

This is not true for children. By maintaining your relationship with your spouse as the first and most important relationship, just after God, you will not only be protecting your marriage, but you will also set a wonderful example for your children.

The most important thing you can do for your children is to

love your spouse openly and honestly in front of them. This creates a home where children feel safe and secure. The importance of modeling a Biblical marriage has generational significance because it gives your children an advantage as they move into their marriage relationship because your children have seen a godly marriage in their own home.

One of the best ways to protect your marriage and maintain your relationship's priority is the establishment of date night. Creating a time for romance to thrive and for you to focus your attention on your spouse reveals their value in the relationship. Establishing a date night before you have children will end up making that night non-negotiable, making certain your spouse remains a top priority in your life.

If you come into a marriage with children, it is crucial that you discuss the blending of your families. You must have a significant discussion on ways you will maintain your spouse as the first and primary relationship, after God, in your life. All children must become OUR children. Therefore, it is important to discuss such topics as discipline, chores, curfews, church attendance, and parenting styles. Birth parents should oversee discipline. Bonus parents are already fighting an uphill battle as the new person.

We recommend you take a course in step-parenting and blended families if you are struggling with blending the two families. This will help you see traps and pitfalls while allowing you to develop a plan for your family.

The blending of two families can be one of the hardest

tasks you will face in a marriage. But by having significant discussions and receiving training, you can increase your likelihood of success tremendously. There are many excellent programs and counselors available. We recommend you seek these services.

Family night is a great way to help blend families. Having time together as a family will allow you to build the bonds of a relationship. A Family Night could include such things as having dinner at the table, promoting conversation, or activities that encourage all members of the family to take part. It can be as simple as playing board games, going for a walk, or working on a project together that would benefit everyone.

It is also important to remember that the blending of families is something that happens over time and often happens much slower than you would like. Many theories show that the blending of families can take as many as seven years to form a new family bond. This, of course, will vary depending on several factors, such as the ages of the children, involvement of birth parents, living arrangements of the children, and the consistency with maintaining parenting standards by both parents.

Chapter 9

Affair-Proofing Your Marriage

W e have spent several chapters talking about specific areas in a marriage that will promote growth. While these are all noble concepts, there is one thing that can undo all your efforts – that is an affair. Affairs are tragic. They can destroy years of trust, steal intimacy, and derail an otherwise healthy sex life. They can undermine finances and break apart families. Affairs are the devil's all-purpose marriage wrecker.

We want to stop affairs before they start. There are not a lot of areas concerning sex that the Bible specifically prohibits, but this is one of them. It is stone-tablet important. When Moses brought down the Ten Commandments in **Exodus 20**, "Thou shalt not commit adultery" was in **verse 14**. The danger of affairs was still present when Jesus said, *"But I tell you that* *anyone who looks at a woman lustfully has already committed adultery with her in his heart."* (**Matthew 5:28**)

The truth of the matter is that the heart is where most affairs start. If that is so, then your spouse's heart becomes the paramount place of importance. You need to make it a priority to protect their heart to ensure the integrity of your marriage. It is often an emotional need or a need for security that leads to extramarital relations. Therefore, we must keep a close eye on our friendships with the opposite sex. Certainly, you should not restrict your friendships to your gender. But be aware that many times having a best friend of the opposite sex, who is not your spouse, can lead to problems.

There is an entire cable channel, the Lifetime Movie Channel, dedicated to stories about best friends who meet the wrong person, marry them, and realize the right person was with them all along. It works great in the movies but is rarely the case in real life. The person you go to when you want to talk about tough topics in life should be the person you gave your ring to.

We have heard things like "I can talk to them about anything," or "they always listen to me." One should be able to say these things about their spouse. If you can't talk to your spouse about things, but can talk to your friend from work, back home, or high school about it, congratulations. You have just introduced secret-keeping to your marriage. You are marrying your spouse because you can share anything with them, and you want to share everything with them. This remains true in a healthy marriage. Remember, stay open, and don't be afraid to share the good, the bad, and the ugly.

A very delicate place to watch for imbalance to sneak into friendship is when couples are good friends with other couples. It is critically important that couples have friends, even mentors that are other couples. It prevents isolation and the problem of only speaking too little ones who still take the bus to school. Adults need other adult relationships.

God designed us for relationships. You need to be mindful of spending more time with your friends or the new couple in your lives, rather than with your spouse. Double dating is great, but it doesn't replace the time when your spouse is the singular focus of your attention.

Whether date night is a fancy dinner, a walk at sunset, or movies and popcorn, it is the two hours where nothing else matters. Being with them helps quench the insecurities that invite others into your position in the relationship. If you have a best friend couple, go out with them, enjoy them, but do it as the group of four. Limit times when you are alone with the opposite sex make it a four-way bond, not a two-way bond.

There are many ways to implement good boundaries in your marriage that neither of you will cross. Let's begin by talking about guarding your eyes. This is an important boundary for guys. Because God designed men to be more visual than women, it is important to set up clear boundaries in this area.

As with everything else, the Bible lays out a clear example

of the destructive power of failing to guard your eyes. **2 Samuel 11:1-5** details one of the most famous elicit romances of all time, the story of David and Bathsheba. It is a story about letting your eyes wander. The problem for David was, where his eyes wandered, he followed.

"In the spring, when kings go forth to battle, David sent Joab with his servants and all Israel, and they ravaged the Ammonites [country] and besieged Rabbah. But David remained in Jerusalem.

One evening, David arose from his couch and was walking on the roof of the king's house. From there, he saw a woman bathing, and she was very lovely to behold. David sent and inquired about the woman.

One said, 'Is not this Bathsheba, the daughter of Eliam and the wife of Uriah the Hittite?' And David sent messengers and took her. And she came into him, and he lay with her—for she was purified from her uncleanness. Then she returned to her house.

And the woman became pregnant and sent and told David, I am with child." (**2 Samuel 11:1-5 AMP**)

Not only did David not guard his eyes, but he also let them gaze upon something or someone they were never intended to see. He also focused on what his eyes saw. Because David did not guard his eyes, but followed them, what he saw led him to a place of sin that was destructive to himself, his family, and Bathsheba's family.

This is a place where daily vigilance must be in place. You

must learn to divert your eyes quickly when you see something that can produce unwanted consequences in your life. Being quick to do this will be helpful. Having someone whom you can discuss this openly with will also help. This is a great place for you to have an accountability partner who will challenge you to remain faithful to your spouse with your eyes.

We also have the choice to focus on what we see. When we allow ourselves time to focus on what we see, we allow that thing to take root in us. It is important to follow the example laid out for us in the book of Job. The Bible says Job made a covenant with his eyes to not look lustfully upon a girl. This is a decision you can make with yourself and with your spouse.

Look at this passage:

"I dictated a covenant (an agreement) to my eyes; how then could I look [lustfully] upon a girl? For what portion should I have from God above [if I were lewd], and what heritage from the Almighty on high? Does not calamity [justly] befall the unrighteous, and disaster the workers of iniquity? Does not [God] see my ways and count all my steps?" (**Job 31:1-4 AMP**)

While your spouse may never know if you chose or not, guard your eyes, you can never fool God. Be proactive from the start. Make a covenant with your eyes. Guard your eyes and avoid the disaster that wandering eyes can bring.

Spending a great deal of time alone is another area that has great potential to lead to problems. There are many reasons one spouse might find himself or herself spending a greater amount of time alone. From jobs, family illness, or traveling, as well as many other reasons, there are times a spouse may have considerable time alone. When this time is constructively used, it provides a fantastic opportunity to build your relationship with God or often even provides time for much-needed rest. However, it also provides the opportunity for problems in your marriage.

Loneliness can be a by-product of prolonged times of separation. This can be something that may drive a spouse to seek ways to eliminate loneliness which can become danger zones. There are also ways to make sure we avoid these danger zones.

One way is by having frequent contact with your spouse during periods of separation. Using text messaging, phone calls, FaceTime, and emails is a great way to stay connected, even if one of you is on the other side of the world. Involvement in church activities will provide a productive outlet to decrease loneliness. Involvement with friends of the same sex is yet another way to ease the negative effects of loneliness.

Discussion of these ideas and planning before encountering these times is vital. Having a specific plan in place will help ensure your marriage thrives.

Physical contact in a way that promotes intimacy is a line that defines whether an emotional affair has changed to a full-blown affair. The common defense is "we are just friends." Do friends hold hands? How long do friend's hug? How often do friends kiss? Do friends ever kiss on the lips?

These may seem like obvious boundaries that are common

sense, however, every act of adultery is a series of choices to go beyond a boundary. It is important to talk about boundaries. Putting those boundaries in place from the beginning will ensure that it does not leave obvious decisions to be made in a moment of weakness.

The following are boundaries that have been proven to be helpful to many couples:

- Never ride alone in a car with a person of the opposite sex who is not a blood relative.
- Never meet with a person of the opposite sex alone in a private place or with doors closed.
- Always allow your spouse access to the passwords of all email/Facebook/Twitter accounts. Allow your spouse full access to your phone at any time.
- Always maintain a relationship with a person to whom you give permission, to ask questions about your behavior, relationship with God, and with your spouse.
- Never share emotional issues with any person of the opposite sex that you haven't previously shared with your spouse.
- Make sure you do all casual texting for informational purposes only, and that your spouse has access to them at all times.

Finally, we want to end with the concept that <u>if the grass</u>

seems greener on the other side of the fence, then you haven't been doing a good job watering and feeding your grass. By making sure you are diligent to treat your marriage as the second most valuable relationship in your life, right behind God, and spending time every day enriching your relationship with your spouse, you will ensure a healthy, happy, and long-lasting marriage.

A concept that has served us well is "whatever you focus on grows." Stay focused on God and your spouse... and watch your marriage grow into something amazing.

Epilogue

In this book, Marriage Made Easy, we have covered a lot of bases, touching on many of the major topics that create issues inside a marriage. We have provided tools that should contribute to a long and healthy relationship.

Over the past ten years of working in a marriage ministry, we have seen more success stories than failures. Whether or not you are a follower of Christ, most of these tools will work for you and you will have a better marriage if you use them.

However, all good structures are built on a solid foundation. For marriage, our foundation is the Lord. God invented marriage. It was His idea and then He wrote a book about it. The Bible starts with a wedding, ends with a wedding, and everything in between is a groom looking for his bride.

So, when we talk about having a great marriage, we need to recognize the Creator of marriage is the best place to learn how to do marriage well. When you do marriage God's way, you have a 100% chance of being successful in your marriage.

Flashback to chapter one: A God-Centered Marriage. Isn't it all about Jesus? At the end of the journey, the best marriage advice we can give is to know Jesus. If you don't know Him as your personal Savior, it's never too late. You will be better for it, your marriage will be better for it, your family will be better for it, and definitely your eternity will be better for it.

If you are in this study and you say that you don't have a personal relationship with God and you have never accepted Jesus as your Savior, then we want to invite you to do that right now.

The Bible says God created the earth, and He created people to fill the earth. Every one of us is born into sin and we live lives separated from God. *"For all have sinned and come short of the glory of God."* (**Romans 3:23**)

The Bible teaches us that the price we will pay for our sin is death unless the Lord intervenes with His gift of life – eternal life. *"For the wages of sin is death but the gift of God is eternal life through Jesus Christ our Lord."* (**Romans 6:23**)

To provide for us a way back to God because He loves us so much, Jesus came to the earth, lived a perfect life, and took our punishment so we could have a relationship with God. We call this being born again. *"But God showed His love toward us, in that, while we were still sinners, Christ died for us."* (**Romans 5:8**)

When you recognize you are a sinner and need a Savior,

the next step is to ask Jesus to be your Savior. *"For whoever calls upon the Name of the Lord will be saved."* (**Romans 10:13**) If you have never done this before, we invite you to make this decision. Simply pray this prayer:

"Jesus, I know I am a sinner. I have done wrong things. Please forgive me for my sin. I believe you died for my sin and rose from the dead. I want to turn from sin and ask you to come into my heart and my life. As you lead me, I will trust you and follow you. Jesus, I receive you as my personal Lord and Savior. I believe I'm saved. I believe my sins are forgiven. Thank you, Jesus, for bringing me back into a relationship with you. Amen."

Now that you have accepted Jesus as your Lord and Savior, we suggest you find a good Bible-believing church and begin your journey to learning more about God, Jesus, and His Word. Your journey with Jesus will deepen as you learn more about Who He is and who He has called you to be. We all need relationships with other believers. If you are doing this study in a group, others around you can help you learn and grow in your relationship with the Lord. Share your decision with them.

If you have a relationship with Jesus, make sure your spouse does too. If you both do, if you both know Jesus, then share how Christ has impacted your marriage with other couples. The reason we wrote this book is that we don't want it to be a secret that:

Marriage is a gift from the Lord!

God loves us. He wants to be in the middle of your marriage for you, your family, and all your friends, whether or not they are married. Marriage, being a type and shadow of Christ and the church, is the best way to show Jesus to those around you.

So, get out there, be married well (You married well, right?), and keep God at the center. As you do this, share Who He is and what He has done for you.

Made in the USA
Columbia, SC
16 September 2024

41860001R00065